SHE KILLS ME

Editor: Samantha Weiner
Managing Editor: Glenn Ramirez
Designer: Jenice Kim
Production Manager: Rachael Marks

Library of Congress Control Number: 2021932572

ISBN: 978-1-4197-4846-2
eISBN: 978-1-64700-000-4

Printed and bound in Thailand
10 9 8 7 6 5 4 3 2 1

Abrams Image books are available at special discounts when purchased in
quantity for premiums and promotions as well as fundraising or
educational use. Special editions can also be created to specification.
For details, contact specialsales@abramsbooks.com or the address below.

ABRAMS The Art of Books
195 Broadway, New York, NY 10007
abramsbooks.com

THE TRUE STORIES OF HISTORY'S

DEADLIEST WOMEN

SHE KILLS ME

JENNIFER WRIGHT

ILLUSTRATIONS BY EVA BEE

Abrams Image, New York

CONTENTS

INTRODUCTION

For every woman in this book, there is an apologist. In the guise of playing the devil's advocate or insisting that you look at all aspects of a situation, someone will always enthusiastically offer an argument in defense of something—or someone—controversial or unpopular.

You can find a report saying that someone talked the Beautiful Beast of Auschwitz, Irma Grese, into torture and murder, and she was just a girl in love. The heroic Soviet aviators, the Night Witches, will be discounted as an urban legend. And there are multiple movies that try to prove the ax murderer Lizzie Borden was innocent. As late as 1998, Roy Hazelwood of the FBI claimed, "there are no female serial killers."

People are very apt to believe that a woman can't kill someone. Not without a man forcing her into it, anyway. Sometimes women contend that these killers must have been framed by the patriarchy. Sometimes men, who conducted some obscure experiment with a Barbie doll and a fork, try to prove women are too weak to pick up swords. I am more inclined to understand the former reasoning since the patriarchy did, in fact, treat women terribly and cavalierly claim they were witches through much of history.

But none of these explanations change the fact that some women commit murder. Maybe for great causes, sometimes for terrible reasons.

If you are reading this, there is a good chance that you are a woman. You are also a person. And as a human, you have felt great anger at some point in your life.

I know you have.

It is something of a dirty secret for women, the fact that we can be very angry. Women shouting or visibly upset, no matter how justified, are dismissed as hysterical. Men scream and rage on podiums and seem manly; women preface reasonable suggestions with "Sorry, I just think that maybe . . . " and conclude by saying "does that make sense?"

For much of history, women have been very good at masking their anger, largely from fear. You can look to the "scold's bridles"—seventeenth-century torture instruments that were fitted over women's heads and their tongues to stop them from speaking when men considered them to be nags. Through the eighteenth and nineteenth centuries it was acceptable for men to decide to imprison "problem wives" in asylums. Do a quick Google search on Elizabeth Packard, who quarreled with her husband and then spent the next three years trying to prove to doctors that she was not insane. Then remember those burned witches, who were generally simply women who lived independently and didn't appear too fond of men and society.

If your life and liberty hinges upon acting sweet, you will comply. We became so good at hiding our feelings that men started to think we didn't feel anger at all. Any instance of female dissent can still seem surprising. That is why men think it is a "scary time" for them when women say, "Hey, stop harassing us at work."

In fact, women are perfectly capable of creating a genuinely scary time for men. The women in this book did. And for the record, a *genuinely* scary time does not mean "women telling men to stop offering them shoulder massages at the office." It means "women will just start poisoning your food."

Some of the deeds in this book are so scary and atrocious that we've noted them in the headers. If you do not want to read about women eating people, that's understandable. If you don't want to live in a world where women occasionally mention that they're not loving shoulder massages, then you're going to be in for a hard time.

There are flames of rage in the heart of every woman, as there are in the heart of every man. Because of the way women have been treated, there is every reason that these urges might burn hotter and brighter. And every so often, there is a woman who acts—and becomes a killer.

To deny women full-throated, murderous anger is to refute that they possess the full range of human emotions. Anger still has a way of seeping out. Let the following women show you moments when it did.

PSYCHOS—BUT NOT THE WAY MISOGYNISTS SAY IT

Yeah, that's right,
women can be horrible people, too.

ELIZABETH BÁTHORY

(1560–1614)

TORTURE + ENSLAVEMENT + JUVENILE DEATH + CANNIBALISM

Countess Elizabeth Báthory couldn't have been better born. She was the niece of the king of Poland and the Prince of Transylvania. Her father was a baron, and she grew up in a castle. She was trained in all manner of studies, and she was known for her attractive appearance. She had it all—wealth, education, beauty. She also had an unparalleled bloodlust that would make her history's most notorious female serial killer.

Elizabeth was no stranger to brutality on her family's Hungarian estates. When she was a child, she watched as a thief was sewn inside the belly of a dying horse. The punishment, which wasn't uncommon, ensured that the thief would struggle to free himself, causing the horse to fight back and guaranteeing maximum displeasure for both. (Even when lying perfectly still, being surrounded by horse guts couldn't have made for a pleasant death.)[1] Rumor has it that Elizabeth delighted at the sight, with some reports going so far as to say that she urinated with excitement.

There were other unnerving childhood experiences. The inbred Elizabeth was spoiled and humored as she dealt with seizures and fits of rage. She was said to be very close to her sadomasochistic aunt and Satanist uncle.

At age fourteen, Elizabeth married Count Ferencz Nádasdy and found herself bored. She could read and write in Hungarian, Latin, and German, but there were few books—a source of irritation to Elizabeth—and little to do at the castle but wait for her husband to return from battle against the Ottomans. She became deeply preoccupied with her looks and took to dressing and redressing constantly, cycling through five or six gowns and sets of jewels each day.[2]

Soon after her marriage, she began torturing her servants, presumably as a means of amusement. Her husband, who shared a similar temperament and who adored his young wife (which seems to put an end to the notion that you have to work to become a lovable person before you can find a partner), reportedly built a torture chamber to her specifications.[3] Free to pursue her passion for deviltry, she sewed one servant girl's mouth shut for talking too much. She forced another to cook and eat her own flesh. She covered some in honey and tied them up outside to be devoured by insects. When it was winter, she opted to pour water on others, leaving them outside to freeze to death.

Some of this may be elaborated for effect, but there's evidence to suggest that Bathory tortured and killed her servants. Sadly, that would not have been an uncommon practice.[4]

---

1. Brenda Ralph Lewis, *The Untold History of the Kings and Queens of Europe* (New York: Cavendish Square, 2016), 29.

2. Valentine Penrose and Alexander Trocchi, *The Bloody Countess: Atrocities of Erzsébet Báthory* (London: Calder Publications, 1970), 43.

3. History.com Editors, "1610—Bathory's Torturous Escapades Are Exposed," History.com, November 13, 2009, https://www.history.com/this-day-in-history/bathorys-torturous-escapades-are-exposed.

4. Susanne Kord, *Murderesses in German Writing, 1720-1860: Heroines of Horror* (United Kingdom: Cambridge University Press, 2009), 61.

But she is best remembered as a proto-vampire. That part of the lore is likely untrue; at least, there's no mention of it at her trial. However, the popular account claims that as a maid was combing her hair too roughly, Elizabeth struck her. Nothing new there. However, when she wiped the maid's blood off her hand, she believed her skin looked smoother and more translucent. Elizabeth slit the girl's throat to use her blood as a kind of lotion. Before long, she was reputedly bathing in the blood of virgins.

Supposedly, Elizabeth's appetite for blood—and murder—proved insatiable. Local girls began to disappear. Before long, the village was essentially empty of potential victims for Báthory. So Elizabeth started a school, encouraging the daughters of lesser nobles to stay with her. When wealthy fathers began wondering why their daughters were dying or vanishing in her care, King Matthias of Hungary finally ordered an investigation. When the castle was raided, fifty girls were found either dead or dying, generally from puncture wounds. A list of six hundred fifty girls' names was also found; a servant told the court the list was a record of Elizabeth's victims.[5]

However, this entire investigation was conducted by the court of Vienna at a time when the court was deeply in debt to Bathory. Finding her guilty of a crime had the potential to eliminate their debt. The servants who confessed did so while being tortured, and many of the over two hundred witnesses brought forward at her trial had little to offer beyond hearsay.

For the next three years Elizabeth was confined to a windowless cell in her castle, her only contact with the outside world through the slits where guards passed her food. She died there at age fifty-four. As far as we can tell, at the end of her life, her skin looked no better nor worse than your average psychotic fifteenth-century middle-aged woman.

The extent of Báthory's crimes is probably exaggerated, likely a product of the misogyny of the times. But that doesn't mean that Bathory, a victim of those times, was incapable of creating her own number of victims.

---

5. Lewis, *The Untold History*, 38.

DELPHINE LALAURIE

(1787–1849)

TORTURE + ENSLAVEMENT + JUVENILE DEATH

Delphine LaLaurie was born to an extremely wealthy, slave-owning family—not a place of great moral high ground. But she managed to sink to depths that surpassed her peers, even during a time when "female slave-owners [were] proverbial for cruelty."[6]

Delphine was known around New Orleans for her charm and her elegant parties, but also for her extreme fits of rage. Some have attributed her cruel treatment of enslaved people to a fear of insurrection among them, since her uncle was killed in a slave uprising. But then, even her children spoke of her bad temper,

---

6. Alexander Marjoribanks, *Travels in North and South America* (New York: D. Appleton and Co., 1853), 365.

claiming they were careful "to avoid anything that might excite *Maman*'s bad mood."[7] It's more likely that enslaved people simply provided an outlet for Delphine's rage, which she knew better than to unleash on white people.

That said, many of Delphine's house guests noted that her slaves looked abnormally malnourished and ill-treated.

As word of Delphine's cruelty began to grow—complaints about her were filed in 1828, 1829, and 1832 by her neighbors—a young lawyer was sent to her house to remind her of the law stipulating that enslaved people able to prove they were cruelly treated could be taken from their masters. The lawyer left their meeting shocked that anyone could believe anything negative about such a refined and delightful woman.

Good looking, wealthy white women get away with a frightening amount of cruelty in America.

Then, a young enslaved girl (some reports claim she was age eight) caught a tangle while she brushed Delphine's hair. Delphine was furious. She chased the child through the house with a whip, until the terrified girl ran off the roof and plummeted to her death, in full view of the neighbors.

This girl, amazingly, was perhaps *better* treated than most of the other enslaved people in Delphine's household.

Her cook was kept chained within eight yards of the stove, even in the broiling Louisiana summer. The cook was not fed. Despite preparing sumptuous dinners for guests, she was starving to death. Finally, in 1834, seemingly deciding that she would rather die than endure this treatment another day, she lit a fire that rapidly spread through the house.

No one, surely, could blame the cook for wanting to burn that place to the ground.

But the blaze alerted the neighbors. As they raced to extinguish the fire they noticed that Delphine was outside—but none of her slaves were beside her. When they went in to fight the flames, the cook shouted at them to save the people locked in the attic. The authorities were called, and they were led up

---

7. Carolyn Morrow Long, *Madame LaLaurie, Mistress of the Haunted House* (Gainesville: University Press of Florida, 2012), loc. 3154 of 5465, Kindle.

to the attic, alongside some onlookers. Once there, they found seven enslaved people chained up. Looking at them, some of the visitors became physically ill. The stench and the sight of the maggots in the enslaved people's wounds alone were surely enough to turn anyone's stomach.

Four years later, in 1838, the sociologist Harriet Martineau wrote, "Of the nine slaves, the skeletons of two were afterwards found poked into the ground; the other seven could scarcely be recognized as human. Their faces had the wildness of famine, and their bones were coming through the skin. They were chained and tied in constrained postures; some on their knees, some with their hands above their heads. They had iron collars with spikes which kept their heads in one position."[8] Next to them could be seen Delphine's whip and the stool she stood upon so as to have a more forceful position from which to beat them.

The lore around Delphine's mistreatment of the people she owned has grown somewhat in its telling over the years. On ghost tours of New Orleans' French Quarter, some say that the slaves' mouths had been stuffed with feces and sewn shut. Others contend that one slave's bones had been broken and reset until they turned into a "human crab." Another story claims that a woman had all her skin peeled off so she resembled a caterpillar. It may say something about some people's insatiable appetite for tales of evil that chaining people in constricted positions, putting spikes around their necks, and allowing them to burn to death in your house is not considered shocking *enough*, and that people made up even more horrific stories about their treatment.

Certainly, at the time the sights were enough for the neighbors to turn on Delphine. In what may be the only time in history when a torch-wielding mob was in the right, the neighbors attempted to destroy the LaLauries' mansion. The house burned, but Delphine and her husband escaped.

Rumor had it they went to Paris. If that's true, then she ended her life in one of the world's most beautiful cities. One can only hope that Delphine LaLaurie, now long dead, is in a place far hotter than that kitchen where she imprisoned her cook.

---

8. Harriet Martineau, *Retrospect of Western Travel*, vol. 2 (London: Saunders and Oatley, 1838), 53.

"JOLLY JANE" TOPPAN
(1854–1938)

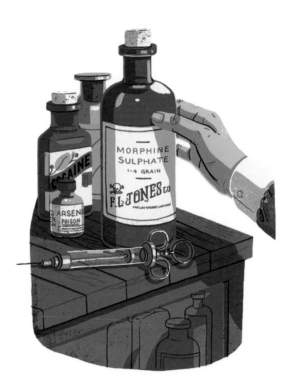

Not everyone who murders has to overcome their natural aversion to it. They're not all killing in self-defense, or because they're bigots who feel some groups deserve it, or because they're blinded by rage.

Some people just like murdering, the way other people enjoy reading or playing tennis. Some people even get a sexual thrill from it.

"Jolly Jane" Toppan was one of those people.

Her nickname was certainly not due to the circumstances of her childhood. Born Honora Kelley, she was the daughter of Irish immigrants. Her mother died of tuberculosis when she was only a year old. Her father, a tailor, sank into a depressive state, which seems like a very polite description of his malady given that he supposedly sewed his own eyes shut.

Not long after, Jane was sent to an orphanage. She was taken in by the Toppan family at the age of five and renamed Jane Toppan.

Her new family treated her more as a servant than a child, expecting her to provide housekeeping services. Still, she had a safe place to stay and was popular and well liked at school. That was true either because of—or in spite of—the fact that she told elaborate lies. She said, for instance, that her father lived in China and that she had a sister who was a famous beauty who had married an English lord. But given the unhappy circumstances of her home life with the Toppans, she could hardly be blamed for preferring a fantasy world to the real one.

For a time she seemed to live a fairly normal life, serving as a housemaid first for the Toppan parents, and then for their daughter, Elizabeth, who was not married to an English lord. But the more horrific aspects of her personality came to light in 1887, when she decided to become a nurse at the age of thirty-three.

Outwardly, Jane was so cheerful during her training that the staff began to call her "Jolly Jane." Many of her patients became fond of her, and she formed close relationships with them—so close that she would give her favorite cured patients small overdoses of medicine to keep them near her in the hospital a few weeks longer.

That was, terrifyingly, the best you could hope for if you were being treated by her. The patients she did not like, she killed.

She began by giving those unfortunate patients overdoses of morphine. Before long she mixed different medications in order to provoke different symptoms, a strategy Jane employed partly because it would make the deaths look accidental, but also because Jane took pleasure in experimenting. It's important to note that she did not kill these patients because they were suffering greatly or expressing a desire to be euthanized. She did not do this out of a sense of mercy. She killed because she liked seeing people die. She liked watching them die in a variety of ways even more. She claimed it produced in her an erotic frisson that she called "voluptuous delight."[9]

---

9. Peter Vronsky, *Female Serial Killers: How and Why Women Become Monsters* (New York: Berkley Publishing Group, 2007), 122.

In 1887 hospital patients died with enough regularity that her crimes didn't strike anyone as especially suspicious. They were more struck by the fact that Jane seemed to be stealing patients' property. Under this cloud, by 1890 she decided to begin working as a private nurse for families who needed in-home care.

She worked primarily for the elderly. That was unfortunate, as she believed "there was no use in keeping old people alive."[10] However, during this period she not only killed the elderly, she also murdered her own adopted sister Elizabeth, watching with relish as she died in her arms.

Afterward, Jane hoped to marry Elizabeth's widower, Oramel Brigham. She proceeded to kill his housekeeper (who she suspected he might marry after Elizabeth died) and his sister. She appeared to think he would definitely marry her as soon as he had no female helpers. This was, in addition to being socio-pathic, not an effective strategy in her case. When Oramel still had no interest in marrying her, she attempted to poison him so she could nurse him back to health. Since (spoiler!) this approach only works in the movie *The Phantom Thread*, her plan failed again.

Jane was ultimately found out only because she foolishly murdered an entire family in 1901. An autopsy found traces of poison in their bodies. Jane was arrested and confessed to at least thirty murders, and possibly as many as a hundred.

Letters poured in from people who couldn't reconcile her cheerful demeanor with her murderous tendencies. At her trial in 1902 she was described as "morally insane." That was a description Jane took issue with, claiming, "I can read a book intelligently, and I don't have bad thoughts, so I don't see where moral degeneracy comes in."[11] On a personal note, I think the moral degeneracy comes in when you start killing people for fun. Jane also said she felt absolutely no guilt or remorse about her actions, which indicates that she was a psychopath.

---

10. Vronsky, *Female Serial Killers*, 128.

11. Nell Darby, "Jolly Jane: (Mis)understanding a Female Serial Killer," *Criminal Historian* (blog), April 14, 2018, http://www.criminalhistorian.com/jolly-jane-misunderstanding-a-female-serial-killer/.

Part of Jane's defense was that she killed because she was an incel. She remarked, "If I had been a married woman, I probably would not have killed all of those people. I would have had my husband, my children, and my home to take up my mind."[12] That was as feeble and stupid a justification then as it is now. If Jane had a family or children, it's far more likely she would have killed them than that they would have cured her psychopathy.

The jury agreed. "Jolly Jane" was found not guilty by reason of insanity. She was committed to an institution where she'd live until her death at age eighty-seven. There, the nurses remember her saying, when the other patients sickened, "Get some morphine, dearie, and we'll go out in the ward. You and I will have a lot of fun seeing them die."[13]

12. "Jolly Jane Toppan, the Killer Nurse Obsessed with Death," New England Historical Society, last modified 2020, http://www.newenglandhistoricalsociety.com/jolly-jane-toppan-killer-nurse-obsessed-death/.

13. Vronsky, *Female Serial Killers*, 134.

CLEMENTINE BARNABET

(1894–?)

In February 1911, a Louisiana paper reported what they called "the most brutal murder in the history of this section."[14] The Byers, a Black family in West Crowley, Louisiana, had been hacked to death. The mother, father, and young son had been found in their bed with an ax wound in each of their heads. A basin filled with blood was in the corner, and bloody tracks marked the floor. The ax was at the head of the bed.

The Byers were the first. They would not be the last.

14. "Brutal Murder of Negro Family Discovered in West Crowley," *The Daily Signal* (Crowley, LA), January 26, 1911, https://www.newspapers.com/clip/12761103/the_daily_signal/.

Less than two weeks later, on February 24, the Andrus family of four, also Black, was similarly slaughtered. Again, the ax rested at the head of the bed.

While murders were common enough in lower-income parts of Louisiana, ax murders were not. The police initially assumed that the murderer must have been motivated by racial hatred. They certainly did not suspect Clementine Barnabet, a seventeen-year-old Black woman running a murder cult.

Based on some suspicions, the police initially assumed that Clementine's father committed the crimes. He had a violent reputation, and more importantly, his demure daughter Clementine told the police she had seen him covered in blood and brains. It is very probable that he would have been found guilty, if another crime had not occurred while he was in jail awaiting trial.

This time, a full suit covered in blood was found in Clementine's room. When it was discovered, Clementine began laughing at the police, which is exactly how you would expect a serial killer to behave in this situation. But Clementine was physically very delicate, and the police couldn't figure out how she could have committed so many murders with an ax, which would have required considerable physical strength. Still, her strange behavior was reason enough for the police to arrest her as well as her brother and two other men.

But the murders continued in Louisiana and then in Texas, even with Clementine in jail.

Soon a spiritual aspect to the murders became apparent. At one home, the Bible inscription "When he maketh the inquest for blood, he forgetteth not the cries of the humble" was found written in blood above the bodies.[15] It was signed "The Human Five."

Due to the religious element in the murders, suspicion fell on a small Pentecostal congregation known as the Church of Sacrifice. Their preacher, Reverend Harris, was arrested.[16] He was released shortly after when he explained that he had no idea how any of his sermons could have inspired such bloody murders. He was likely as confused by Clementine's actions as the Beatles would have been by Charlie Manson.

---

15. Alan G. Gauthreaux and D. G. Hippensteel, *Dark Bayou: Infamous Louisiana Homicides* (Jefferson, NC: McFarland and Company, 2016), 57.

16. "Ask Commission to Examine Ax Woman," *The Crowley Signal* (Crowley, LA), October 26, 1912.

If there was any truly bloodthirsty cult at work, Clementine appeared to be its leader. In April of 1912, she made a full confession, admitting to the murder of at least seventeen people by her own hand. She explained that she had dressed in male clothing and hopped aboard trains to commit the murders, and rather more disturbingly, she had lain in the beds and fondled the corpses. Clementine also claimed that she had numerous followers, including her brother and father, who she incited to commit murders on her behalf. She also said that her followers were unafraid of being caught because of voodoo charms offering them protection.[17]

After Clementine's confession, the *Mitchell Commercial* reported, "As many women belonged to the cult as men, and they shared equally with the men in the sacrifice of human lives."[18] I suppose, in that regard, you could say they really struck a blow for equality.

Still, perhaps Clementine wasn't entirely wrong about her followers being protected. Despite several attempts to find and arrest them in the following years, most of them (if they existed) were never found. Murders continued until 1913, and then ceased without explanation.

As for Clementine herself, people were certain that she would be sentenced to the death penalty. Instead, perhaps again because death seemed too harsh a fate to mete out to such a young woman, she was sentenced to life in Angola State Penitentiary. Ten years later she simply walked out. No one knows how this happened, but it's only one part of the enduring mystery surrounding her.

Because where she walked *to* is also largely unknown. The closest we have to any information about what became of her came from 2002, when a woman called Voodoogal11 recalled her grandmother telling her the story of Clementine, "a Black woman so beautiful with alabaster skin and eyes so piercing she would look at you and turn you to stone."[19] It was only when she attended the funeral in the 1980s and saw pictures of her grandmother as a young woman that she realized her grandmother *was* Clementine Barnabet.

17. Mara Bovsun, "Who Do the Voodoo and the Church of Sacrifice," *New York Daily News*, June 9, 2019, https://www.nydailynews.com/news/crime/ny-justice-story-ax-woman-20190609 -qf5yebikjvhj7bok5odmnzoboq-story.html.

18. "Bloody Cult Confesses to Murder of Forty Negroes," *The Mitchell Commercial* (Mitchell, IN), April 11, 1912, https://newspaperarchive.com/mitchell-commercial-apr-11-1912-p-1/.

19. Gauthreaux and Hippensteel, *Dark Bayou*, 63.

IRMA GRESE

(1923-1945)

TORTURE + ENSLAVEMENT

Later in this book I am going to praise, loudly and at length, some women who killed Nazis. Living as we do in an age where we are expected to be respectful of all and refrain from punching those who seem to actively embrace Nazism, you may feel I am being unfair. In that case, allow me to direct you to the depravations of Nazi Irma Grese.

Irma, sometimes referred to as "the beautiful beast of Belsen" and the "hyena of Auschwitz,"[20] was a member of the SS (*Schutzstaffel*), the so-called

---

20. Lauren Willmott, "The Real 'Beast of Belsen'? Irma Grese and Female Concentration Camp Guards," *History Today*, June 1, 2015, https://www.historytoday.com/history-matters/real-beast-belsen-irma-grese-and-female-concentration-camp-guards.

"elite corps" of the Nazi Party. The SS were in charge of overseeing concentration camps orchestrating the "final solution" —which is better known now as the holocaust. Irma began her work as a guard at the Auschwitz concentration camp in 1942 and transferred to Bergen-Belsen as warden of the women's section in 1945. In those already cruel concentration camps she was known for her *extreme* cruelty.

It takes a lot for an SS guard to stand out as *especially* awful given that the job involved working prisoners to death, killing them immediately in gas chambers, or injecting poison into their veins. But Irma managed.

Female guards rarely committed murder directly. They were sometimes seen as slightly more merciful than their male counterparts. Many weren't even devoted members of the Nazi Party—just local women who wanted a steady job. (As an aside, think for a moment about how poorly regarded these people are remembered in history if you ever feel pressured to take a job that strikes you as immoral.) Irma did not fit this mold. She liked her work. Although she was under little external pressure to do so, Irma reportedly turned the women's camp at Auschwitz into a "sadistic playground."[21]

Nothing in her past indicated that would be the case. Irma had grown up on a farm, the prototypical blonde, fresh-faced country fräulein the Nazis admired. She had aspired, but failed, to become a nurse. One prisoner from Auschwitz, Vera Alexander, told PBS, "I thought she was a small silly country bumpkin. She became someone just because she was wearing a uniform and had a whip in her hand."[22]

She became depraved. Fania Fénelon, one survivor of the camps who wrote about her experiences in her memoir *Playing for Time*, noted, "The women had learned to dread the penalty of her attentions, the least of which meant a whip lash on the nipple."[23] When the wounds predictably became infected, Grese liked to watch as the "doctors" at Auschwitz "operated" on them.

21. *Auschwitz: Inside the Nazi State,* "Corruption," PBS, accessed January 16, 2021, https://www.pbs.org/auschwitz/about/transcripts_4.html.

22. *Auschwitz,* "Corruption," accessed January 16, 2021.

23. Fania Fénelon, *Playing for Time* (Syracuse, NY: Syracuse University Press, 1997).

Irma was one of the few women allowed to carry a gun, and she did not hesitate to use it on the female prisoners at Auschwitz. Vera Alexander noted, "She shot one woman dead who was standing in front of me. Her brains landed on my shoulder. The next day, after the selections, Irma came to see me. I refused to talk to her. She asked, 'Are you angry with me?' I replied, 'You nearly killed me yesterday.' She answered: 'One down, it doesn't matter.'"[24]

It truly did not matter to Irma. Witnesses at the camp said she would beat women for inconsequential matters, such as "wearing the wrong shoes, or stockings."[25] She shot two women who were attempting to escape from a gas chamber. She set her starving dog on prisoners to maul or kill them. (I find myself wishing, among other things, that she had not dragged a dog into her actions, for all dogs are naturally good.)

After the war, Irma was one of only three female guards to be sentenced to death. She was executed in December 1945 with her last word being "quickly."[26] Former concentration camp prisoners were issued a special pass to witness her hanging.[27]

And then she died.

To which I'd say—"One down."

24. *Auschwitz*, "Corruption," accessed January 16, 2021.

25. "Belsen Woman Guard Shot Two Women," *The Berkshire Eagle* (Berkshire County, MA), September 25, 1945.

26. Cynthia Southern, "Irma Grese: The Blonde Beast of Birkenau and Belsen," Warfare History Network, December 29, 2018, https://warfarehistorynetwork.com/2018/12/29/irma-grese-the-blonde-beast-of-birkenau-and-belsen/.

27. "Eleven Executed as British Chief Denies Appeals," *Chippewa Falls Herald* (Chippewa Falls, WI), December 14, 1945.

HOW TO SPOT A PSYCHOPATH

If you are worried that you are a psychopath, good news! Likely you are not. Lucy Foulkes noted in the *Guardian* that many people show periodic instances of psychopathic traits, but one of the defining characteristics of a true psychopath is that they are "entirely unconcerned with the effect their behavior has on others." So, in somewhat circuitous reasoning, if you are worried that you have this personality disorder, you're fine.

If you are concerned that someone you know is a psychopath, and you want to spot them before they kill you, these are some identifying traits:

- CRUEL TO ANIMALS. MOST DIAGNOSED PSYCHOPATHS TORTURE AND KILL ANIMALS IN THEIR YOUTH.[28]

- SUPERFICIALLY CHARMING, WITHOUT FEELING ANY EMOTIONAL ATTACHMENT TO THOSE WITH WHOM THEY TALK.[29]

- BELIEVE THEY ARE SUPERIOR TO OTHER PEOPLE.[30]

- DO WHAT THEY WANT, WITHOUT REGARD FOR LAWS OR MORALITY.[31]

- HAVE LOW IMPULSE CONTROL AND TEND TO ENGAGE IN RISKY BEHAVIORS, LIKE UNPROTECTED SEX OR SUBSTANCE ABUSE.[32]

---

28. Jon Ronson, *The Psychopath Test: A Journey Through the Madness Industry* (New York: Riverhead Books, 2012), 117.

29. Ronson, *The Psychopath Test*, 112.

30. Melissa Burkley, "3 Key Traits That May Be Red Flags for Psychopathy," *Psychology Today*, January 8, 2018, https://www.psychologytoday.com/us/blog/the-social-thinker/201801/3-key-traits-may-be-red-flags-psychopathy.

31. Lucy Foulkes, "The Psychopath in You," *The Guardian*, June 10, 2016, https://www.theguardian.com/science/head-quarters/2016/jun/10/the-psychopath-in-you-psychopathic-traits-spectrum.

32. Ronson, *The Psychopath Test*, 99.

- HAVE BEEN IN LEGAL TROUBLE.[33]

- LIE FREQUENTLY.[34]

- HAVE TROUBLE IDENTIFYING EMOTIONS—SUCH AS FEAR— FROM FACIAL EXPRESSIONS.[35]

- TAKE PLEASURE FROM CAUSING OTHERS PAIN.[36]

- CAN FEEL LONELINESS OR SADNESS, BUT NOT MUCH ANXIETY OR GUILT.[37]

33. Foulkes, "The Psychopath in You."

34. Ally Foster, "The Common Trait That People with 'Dark' Tendencies Share," News.com.au, September 28, 2018, https://www.news.com.au/lifestyle/health/mind/the-common-trait-that-people-with-dark-tendencies-share/news-story/91327ebb058c62cf6d5125696ca4425c.

35. Jesse Bering, "The Problem with Psychopaths: A Fearful Face Doesn't Deter Them," *Scientific American*, September 29, 2009.

36. Foster, "The Common Trait That People with 'Dark' Tendencies Share."

37. Ronson, *The Psychopath Test*, 114.

PRETTY POISONERS

*"Making poison is as much fun as making a cake.
People like to make poison. If you don't understand
this, you will never understand anything."*

—Margaret Atwood

LOCUSTA OF GAUL
(DIED 69 CE)

JUVENILE DEATH + RAPE

It's good to have work you're respected for. Women have worked forever, no matter what memes fetishizing the 1950s try to tell you. It's just that, with rare exceptions, like Queens, their jobs were often confined to the home, toiling as maids, as cooks, or as governesses. It was less common that a woman might find a job outside the home that could elevate her financially and socially.

You should not become a professional poisoner. But it did seem to work for Locusta of Gaul, Rome's most famous poisoner, often described as history's first serial killer. (Although, as far as I can tell, her motives were entirely merce-nary, and, unlike most serial killers, she derived no thrills from her kills.)

Born in the countryside of Gaul, Locusta grew up learning about herbs and botany, including the benefits and the dangers of certain plants. Upon moving to Rome she realized that the quickest way to turn a profit from that knowledge was to provide people with poisons. In a city where greed and ambition were rampant, and everyone had plenty of enemies, she found no shortage of customers.

Brisk sales did not mean she was immune from the law. Locusta was imprisoned and might have died an early death had word of her skills not reached Empress Agrippina the Younger. In 54 CE Agrippina wished to murder her husband Claudius, the better to ensure her son Nero inherited the throne. And so, she decided to employ Locusta.

First, Locusta supplied a poison intended to agitate the bowels of Claudius's guard and food tester. With him out of the way, poison was spread onto a dish of mushrooms, Claudius's favorite food. He ate them without hesitation. However, being a cautious man, Claudius always had a feather on hand. In the event he suspected poison, he could use the feather to tickle the back of his throat and make himself vomit.

His plan failed.

Because Locusta saw to it that the feather had also been soaked in poison.

Agrippina wasn't the only member of the family to employ Locusta's skills. Nero seemingly didn't feel his mother's machinations had been sufficient to ensure he kept the throne permanently. He recruited Locusta to provide poison to kill his brother (and competitor for the throne) Britannicus.

The murder took significant skill. Poison could not simply be poured into Britannicus's food or drink, as everything was sampled by a food tester. If the poison was quick acting, the food tester would die almost instantly, leaving his employer unharmed. If the poison was slow acting, the fact that both the food tester and his employer became sick could serve as proof that they had been poisoned, hopefully casting suspicion upon the killer. Both instances needed to be avoided.

So, at a party, Britannicus was presented with a goblet of wine that was extremely hot, but utterly harmless. The food taster tried it and emerged unharmed. But Britannicus quickly began gasping, and "speechless, he stopped breathing."[1]

The poison was not in the wine. It was in the carafe of cold water that Britannicus used to lower the temperature of his wine. As he died in front of the party, gasping for breath, Nero told everyone that his brother often suffered from such epileptic fits.

Nero is remembered as a truly evil, insane emperor. But Locusta did well by him. He freed her from prison, appointed her "Imperial Poisoner," and granted her large estates. Perhaps more importantly, he also issued a pardon for the many poisonings she had committed. She spent what I assume were a happy few years murdering people at the direction of the imperial family and even opened a school to teach others how to make poisons.

Not bad for a peasant girl from Gaul.

But her contentment was brief. The citizens revolted against Nero, and the Senate condemned him. That was understandable, as he was always killing people—including his mother, Agrippina, who had once been so desperate to see him on the throne. (When Nero's assassins came for her, she ruefully told them they should stab her in her womb.) Nero committed suicide in 68 CE. Sadly for him, he did so without the aid of Locusta's poisons. Nero's successor, Emperor Galba, very quickly and very sensibly arrested Nero's cronies and sentenced them to death.

An enduring myth regarding Locusta is that a specially trained giraffe raped her to death. Given the Romans' love of animal punishments, that doesn't sound *entirely* unlikely. However, it's more probable she was dispatched in a less outlandish fashion. Cassius Dio writes, "Locusta, the sorceress, and others of the scum that had come to the surface in Nero's day, he [Galba] ordered them to be led in chains throughout the whole city and then to be executed."[2]

So while it's not accurate to say "crime doesn't pay"—it does, that is indeed one of the main reasons people commit crimes—in some cases, like Locusta's, it only pays very briefly. And God help you if giraffes find out about your misdeeds.

---

1. Tacitus, *The Annals* (New York: The Modern Library, date 1942), Book XIII, 15.

2. Cassius Dio, Book LXIII, Loeb Classical Library edition (Cambridge, MA: Harvard University Press, 1925), 63.3.

GIULIA TOFANA

(CA. 1620–1659)

TORTURE

There was a time when the worst thing that could happen to a marriage was not "it ends in divorce." Couples for much of history were bound together, sometimes very unhappily, until death.

And while being bound in that manner meant that some couples might have rekindled their love, others just went ahead and killed each other.

Unable to gain employment or generally hold property, there are many women in history who realized that widowhood might be their best route to some kind of freedom. That was a path Giulia Tofana was happy to escort women down during the 1600s.

Giulia was born in Palermo. Her mother Thofania d'Adamo was executed for murdering her husband in 1633.[3] She left to her daughter Giulia the recipe for a poison that would be employed so effectively it would become known as Aqua Tofana.[4] Brilliantly disguised as a cosmetic (to allay men's suspicion), the poison was a mix of arsenic, lead, and belladonna. Each of those ingredients is deadly on their own. Together they could kill a man with as few as four drops. At the first drop, a man might experience symptoms similar to those of a cold. With the second, he could become flu-like. With the third, he'd be bedridden, and with the fourth, he'd be dead.[5]

The poison's greatest asset was that it was remarkably hard to detect, as was reported in one magazine in the 1890s:

> *To save her fair fame, the wife would demand a post-mortem examination. Result, nothing—except that the woman was able to pose as a slandered innocent, and then it would be remembered that her husband died without either pain, inflammation, fever, or spasms. If, after this, the woman within a year or two formed a new connection, nobody could blame her; for, everything considered, it would be a sore trial for her to continue to bear the name of a man whose relatives had accused her of poisoning him.[6]*

Just like that, an unhappy wife could be free.

Giulia was herself a widow, so it's quite possible that she had personal knowledge of the poison her mother created. If she wanted to break out of her marriage, as her mother had, she was not alone.

Business was very brisk for Giulia. So busy, in fact, that she was estimated to have contributed to the deaths of six hundred people. Multiple associates,

3. Genevieve Carlton, "Meet the Woman Who Poisoned Makeup to Help Over 600 Women Murder Their Husbands," Weird History, *Medium*, March 2, 2018, https://medium.com/@editors_91459/meet-the-woman-who-poisoned-makeup-to-help-over-600-women-murder-their-husbands-cfb03929c36d.

4. "Aqua Tofana," extract from the *British Medical Journal*, December 25, 1909, *Medical Review of Reviews* 16 (1910): 103, https://babel.hathitrust.org/cgi/pt?id=mdp.39015011417097&view=1up&seq=109.

5. Don Rauf, *Historical Serial Killers* (New York: Enslow Publishing, 2015), 57.

6. "Tofana, the Italian Poisoner," *Ballou's Monthly Magazine*, volume 72 (July-December 1890), 309-11, https://babel.hathitrust.org/cgi/pt?id=nyp.33433081756086&view=1up&seq=319.

including Giulia's own daughter, soon began helping to prepare and sell the potions, which were hidden in vials emblazoned with the image of Saint Nicholas of Bari, a figure who would provide the inspiration for Santa Claus.

Think twice the next time you get a can of Coke with Santa's image on the side. Historically, that signified poison.

How Giulia's reign of terror—or female emancipation—came to an end is in dispute. We know that, "in the year 1659 during the reign of Pope Alexander VII, it was observed in Rome that many young married women were left widows, and that many husbands died when they became disagreeable to their wives."[7] Certainly, people were on to her and her associates by then.

Some claim that Giulia died in 1651, peacefully in her bed.[8] Others say she was turned in by a woman who was overcome with guilt after nearly feeding her husband poisoned soup.[9]

Still others claim that as more and more husbands died, suspicion fell upon her and Giulia sought refuge in a convent. The people initially rioted to protect Giulia. But when authorities spread a rumor that she had been poisoning wells, sentiment turned against her, and she met her demise. "Dragged from the convent where she'd been hiding, she was tortured and strangled, and her corpse was thrown over the wall into the garden of the convent."[10]

The poison outlived Giulia. On his deathbed in 1791, Mozart was heard moaning that someone had used Aqua Tofana to murder him. It was more likely he died of syphilis, but the fact that he could still see Giulia Tofana's ghostly hand reaching through the ages is a wonderfully terrifying image.

Today, Giulia and her poison are largely forgotten. But if your husband becomes too disagreeable, you may want to remind him they existed.

---

7. "Beckmann's *A History of Inventions and Discoveries*," *The Quarterly Review*, volume 28 (London: John Murray, 1816), 423, https://books.google.co.uk/.

8. Mike Dash, "Aqua Tofana: Slow-Poisoning and Husband-Killing in 17th-Century Italy," *A Blast from the Past* (blog), April 6, 2015, https://mikedashhistory.com/2015/04/06/aqua-tofana-slow-poisoning-and-husband-killing-in-17th-century-italy/.

9. Carlton, "Woman Who Poisoned Makeup."

10. David Stuart, *Dangerous Garden: The Quest for Plants to Change Our Lives* (Cambridge, MA: Harvard University Press, 2004), 120.

CATHERINE MONVOISIN
(1640–1680)

JUVENILE DEATH

Witches aren't real.

When we refer to something as a "witch hunt," we do so to indicate the absurdity of the persecution. After all, witches don't exist.

OK, *some* do, but those self-identified witches are generally kindly pagans who are very in touch with nature. The worst they're going to do is overcharge you for a crystal.

But we will still deny the existence of the all-powerful, black arts practicing witches of fiction, unless . . . well, unless they're Catherine Monvoisin.

There's always at least one exception to the rule.

Catherine Deshayes began life as a homeless girl. At nine, she started telling fortunes for money. She was uncommonly good at it, talented enough to amass a fairly substantial fortune. By age twenty, she had married a jeweler, Antoine Monvoisin, and retired, but after his business went bankrupt, she returned to her trade. A rival claimed, "before she got up every morning, there were folks waiting to see her, and throughout the rest of the day she was with more people, after that, she kept open house in the evening with violins playing, and was always making merry."[11] She performed palm readings and face readings . . . as well as abortions.

To those who think that her financial load might have been lessened without supporting her husband—she tried to kill him multiple times. So great was her loathing for him that, "the standard form of polite greeting upon meeting her was to enquire whether her husband had yet died."[12]

For most of her clients she attempted to engineer somewhat happier outcomes, and she traded primarily in love potions. Those potions were not, as one might imagine, sugar and spice and all things nice, but rather they were composed of "bones of toads, the teeth of moles, cantharides (also known as Spanish fly, a type of emerald green beetle), iron filings, human blood, and human dust."[13] People will do a lot for love. Including murder.

Catherine found the French court was full of people who wanted to kill their spouses so they could run off with their lovers. And thought she was outwardly pious and apt to declare that she'd been given her psychic gifts by God, Catherine was more than willing to provide poison and perform what she regarded as darker magic to help these clients, especially aristocrats willing to offer a great deal of money.

---

11. Anne Somerset, *The Affair of the Poisons: Murder, Infanticide, and Satanism at the Court of Louis XIV* (New York: St Martin's Press, 2014), 152.

12. Somerset, *Affair of the Poisons*, 152.

13. Don Rauf, *Historical Serial Killers* (New York: Enslow Publishing, 2015), 59.

One of the aristocratic ladies who came to Catherine was Madame de Montespan, Louis XIV's mistress. In 1667 she hired her to perform a "black mass" to the devil to ensure she won King Louis XIV's love. At such ceremonies, de Montespan was said to serve as a "living altar" to the devil, and the blood of a baby (likely procured from one of the abortions Catherine performed) was poured over her. This does not seem as if it would bring about anyone's love, but from de Montespan's perspective, the black mass was successful. Madame de Montespan did become the King's mistress (and bore him seven children).

Madame de Montespan continued to see Catherine for aphrodisiacs she used to drug the King. This sounds terrible, but again, from Montespan's perspective, everything went well until 1679 when the King grew tired of her. Around that time, he began sleeping with Marie Angélique de Scorailles, Duchess of Fontanges.

When this relationship came to de Montespan's attention, she decided to kill him. Naturally, she enlisted Catherine's help, as she had so many times in the past. But this time, Catherine was not as successful. She covered a pamphlet to be distributed to the King with poison. But, as there was an excess of people attempting a royal audience on the day it was to be delivered, it never reached him. Catherine resolved to try again.

But before she was able to succeed, people came to suspect that King Louis's sister-in-law had been poisoned. Remarkably, that had nothing to do with Catherine, but the incident led public sentiment to turn against sorceresses and poisoners.

Catherine's arrest in December of 1679 seemed inevitable. There was some hesitancy to arrest her because people feared she would expose too many noblemen and women. But during her trial, Catherine (who was seemingly very drunk at all of her interrogations) expended most of her efforts on defaming her rival, Marie Bosse.

Catherine eventually confessed to a number of crimes and named various accomplices. She was convicted of witchcraft, and on February 22, 1680, she was burnt at the stake. It was then estimated she was responsible for the deaths of over a thousand people.

Much of the episode was hushed up by King Louis XIV, who did not wish for his judgment to be questioned once his longtime mistress was revealed to be a Satanist who wanted to murder him. Madame de Montespan remained at court for a surprising amount of time, considering she'd tried to poison the King.

CHRISTIANA EDMUNDS

(1828–1907)

JUVENILE DEATH

As for Madame Monvoisin, her story remains one of the only times in history when a witch hunt involved an actual witch.

The notion of an evil hag poisoning waifs with an apple only works if people want to eat apples. By the 1900s, they had to use something far more tempting.

Enter Christiana Edmunds, the Chocolate Cream Killer.

Christiana was one of the few poisoners who killed for love, not money. In 1871, the thirty-something Brighton woman developed a crush on her doctor, Charles Beard. She lived a solitary life tending to her aged mother, but she sent him many letters. Dr. Beard was happily married, and he assumed Christiana's affection probably just stemmed from a need for friendship. He remarked, "You must be a bit lonely in that big house. Would you like my wife and I to call on you occasionally?"[14] Christiana replied that she would, and Dr. Beard suggested that she "drop in on my wife some afternoon and introduce yourself."

I'm sure Dr. Beard felt good about this kindly action, but only for a very brief time.

Christiana did indeed go to see Mrs. Beard. Shortly after their visit, Dr. Beard returned home from work and was greeted by his wife, ill and shaking with fear. She told him that Christiana Edmunds had tried to poison her. Christiana, she explained, had given her a chocolate that tasted so unnatural she spat it out immediately. Her husband investigated the gob of remaining candy and found that it was filled with poisonous strychnine. He promptly went to Christiana to ask her what the hell she was doing and to inform her that he was going to the police. Christiana claimed that she had no idea what he was referring to, and that she must have bought some poisoned candy.

This, obviously, was a terrible defense. But it worked. Dr. Beard agreed not to report her to the police.

And throughout the spring and summer of 1871, a lot of people *did* get sick from the candy they bought at Maynard's, the local candy shop. "A metallic taste in the mouth was the first sign that something was wrong, followed by a burning sensation in the throat, vomiting and muscle spasms."[15]

Then, on June 12, a four-year-old boy named Sidney Barker was given a bag of candies from the Maynard store by his uncle. He ate the candies, and within an hour he was convulsed in agony. He died before the doctor could arrive.

Suspicion naturally fell upon the owner of Maynard's, especially as Christiana had sent letters advising people to take legal action against him. It was around that time, however, that the police noticed Christiana had been buying a

---

14. "Case of the Poisoned Candy," *San Francisco Examiner*, January 28, 1951.

15. David Shariatmadari, "Arsenic Was Their Poison—We Have Tobacco, Guns and Sugar," *The Guardian*, March 18, 2016, https://www.theguardian.com/commentisfree/2016/mar/18/poison-arsenic-gun-control-crime.

lot of strychnine, the same poison found in the chocolates. She rather foolishly had the poison hand-delivered to her house, and she was thus easily identified.

The police soon deduced that, in what must be the world's most terrible attempt at a cover-up, Christiana had been buying up chocolates, injecting them with poison, and then returning them to Maynard's store. She hoped that by doing so she would show Dr. Beard that she had not intended to murder his wife, and that this proof would cause the two of them to fall in love and run away together.

It emphatically did not.

Some people speculated that Dr. Beard and Christiana Edmunds *were* having an affair, as if this might exonerate her. To that I'm inclined to reply: Maybe they were, but plenty of people have affairs without killing anyone. Moreover, this is one of the rare cases of "that lady was crazy" rhetoric where I am inclined to agree that she was actually delusional, given that she poisoned a toddler with chocolates.

At her trial in 1872 Edmunds was deemed insane and thus escaped execution. This was enough to pique some reporters, such as those at the *Pall Mall Gazette* who noted that Christiana's crime was monstrous, that she seemed to know what she was doing when she was committing it, and that she had a motive. They suspected "she is to be reprieved for the far simpler reason that she is a woman, and not a man."[16]

In spite of their concerns, Christiana was sent to the Broadmoor Lunatic Asylum, where she remained until her death in 1907. Until that time, she continued to proclaim her love for Dr. Beard. It's safe to say he never sent her chocolates.

---

16. *The Pall Mall Gazette* (London), January 24, 1872.

TILLIE KLIMEK

(1876–1936)

The easiest way to know the future is to create it.

Ottilie (Tillie) Klimek figured that out.

Tillie was born in Poland in 1876, and her parents emigrated to Chicago when she was around one year old. As a child she showed herself to be an excellent cook (especially of stew). She also claimed to have psychic gifts and an ability to predict the future. The quality of the stew was easy to verify. The psychic gifts, less so.

She was, however, stunningly accurate regarding the dates her husbands were going to die.

Tillie married her first husband, John Mitkiewicz, in 1890, when she was only fourteen. In 1914, she told a friend that she had a dream that foretold him dying on a specific date. Cara Davidson, one of her biographers, writes, "When John fell sick on that exact day and died later that night, her friend was awestruck."[17] But then, Tillie had an uncommon advantage when it came to predicting the date. She had been mixing arsenic into his food.

After walking away from her first marriage with one thousand dollars in life insurance money, she quickly wed Joseph Ruskowski. Just as she had with her first husband, she predicted the day of his death, much impressing her neighbors. This time, she didn't wait twenty-five years. He died in May 1914, at which time Tillie received seven hundred dollars from his life insurance policy.

To lose one husband may be a misfortune; to lose two looks like you might be poisoning them. Tillie's next lover, Joseph Guszkowski, was suspicious. When he failed to propose on a romantic weekend, she told him that she had murdered men for less. He threatened to expose her "arsenic tendencies,"[18] at which point she foretold his death to him. You would think that, knowing this he might have been able to avoid it. He didn't. His death came to pass, just like her previous predictions.

It wasn't long before Tillie married again. Her next husband, Frank Kupczyk, was a great fan of her vegetable soup. She quickly began taunting him with predictions of his death. She even asked her landlady to allow her to store a thirty-dollar coffin (a bargain!) in the building, explaining her husband wouldn't be alive much longer. By this point, "hundreds believed she was possessed of supernatural powers,"[19] which seems extraordinary, given that the much simpler

---

17. Cara Davidson, *Black Widow Tillie Klimek* (CreateSpace Independent Publishing Platform, 2016), loc. 53 of 284, Kindle.

18. Davidson, *Black Widow*, loc. 80.

19. Tori Telfer, "Lady Killers: Tillie Klimek, High Priestess of the Bluebeard Clique," Jezebel, January 7, 2015, https://jezebel.com/lady-killers-tillie-klimek-high-priestess-of-the -blue-1677860528.

explanation for why a woman was able to predict the death of four men is *she was poisoning them*.

She left that marriage $675 richer, but with people in the community increasingly adverse to meeting with her, as they feared having their own deaths predicted.

Tillie met her next husband at Frank's funeral. Joseph Klimek was a fifty-year-old man who claimed that he married Tillie "for a home."[20] She gave him one, complete with her signature meals, sprinkled with arsenic provided by her cousin.

Joseph was the first to survive Tillie's poisoned meals, though he was partially paralyzed afterward. People found it suspicious not that *he* had sickened and almost died, but that his two dogs had become ill at the same time. The police began looking into the matter. In the course of their investigation, they talked to a clerk who said Tillie had recently bought a mourning dress. "Who died?" the clerk had asked her. "My husband," she replied. "I'm sorry," the clerk said, "When did he die?" She replied, "Ten days from now."[21]

The police questioned Tillie, and she confessed to poisoning Joseph's food, explaining "he was fooling around with other women and I wanted to get rid of him."[22] Initially, she insisted her other husbands had died of natural causes, but when the body of one of her former husbands was exhumed, it was found to be full of arsenic.

A trial, with massive publicity, quickly commenced.

Given that this woman managed to marry four times, despite murdering people (or as some would say, "having a bad personality"), you could be excused for wondering if she was super hot. She was not. Which is a shame, as her outcome likely would have been better if she was. Young and attractive Jazz Age murderesses were often found not guilty, in part because male jurors were besotted. But Tillie wasn't a beautiful twenty-something flapper who killed her husband in a

---

20. Telfer, "Lady Killers."

21. Joseph McNamara, "Black Widow Killings," *New York Daily News*, September 13, 1992.

22. "Hostess of Poison Banquets Gets Life for Her Crimes," *New York Daily News*, July 5, 1925.

jealous rage. She was forty-five and, as the *New York Daily News* reporter wrote, "A crude, unattractive, uneducated woman."[23]

Finding no sympathetic jurors, she was sentenced to life for her crimes, prompting the *Chicago Daily Tribune*'s Genevieve Forbes to claim that, in an impressively sexist quip, "Tillie Klimek went to the penitentiary because she never went to the beauty parlor."[24]

But her homeliness had not hindered her ability to marry—repeatedly. Perhaps it's true that the way to a man's heart is through his stomach. Especially if you want to stop his heart from beating. But then, I suppose we all could have predicted that.

---

23. "Hostess of Poison Banquets," *New York Daily News*.
24. Al Cimino, *Women Who Kill: A Chilling Casebook of True-Life Murders* (London: Arcturus Publishing, 2019), chapter 28.

POISONING HUSBANDS

In 1851, the British House of Lords attempted to ban women from buying arsenic as too many were using it to poison their husbands.

Truly, it was a scary time for men in England. Not only were women pushing for better workplace conditions, and beginning to suggest they'd like to vote, now men feared their wives were going to poison them, largely for being awful. At the time, a woman was considered a man's property, and he had full control of her earnings, land, and children. If the man became abusive, a woman had very little recourse, and if she fled, she would have to relinquish her children and all her property to her abusive husband. Widowhood was more or less the *only* way to achieve financial and social independence.

And, so, poison. Women often weren't sufficiently physically strong to outright murder their husbands, but they could easily slip a dose of arsenic into his food or drink. It was virtually undetectable, and the symptoms, like diarrhea or vomiting, were also found in countless diseases of the time.[25] If you were found out, since it was a white odorless substance you could easily say you just stupidly mistook it for salt or sugar.[26]

In the years between 1843 and 1851, sixteen Englishwomen were found guilty of poisoning family members with arsenic.[27] That is not, admittedly, a *huge* number. However, despite the fact that 90 percent of spousal homicides were committed by men,[28] the Earl of Carlisle became so concerned he slipped a clause into the Sale of Arsenic Regulation Bill stating, "arsenic should be sold to none but male adults."[29] The House of Lords initially accepted this amendment,

25. Joan Acocella, "Murder by Poison," *New Yorker*, October 7, 2013, https://www.newyorker.com /magazine/2013/10/14/murder-by-poison.

26. Robin Lindley, "Arsenic: Victorians' Secret," *Crosscut*, September 2, 2010, https://crosscut .com/2010/09/arsenic-victorians-secret.

27. Richard Clark, "Arsenic poisoning," *Capital Punishment UK* (blog), accessed January 16, 2021, http:// www.capitalpunishmentuk.org/arsenic.htm.

28. Lindley, "Arsenic: Victorians' Secret."

29. Sandra Hempel, *The Inheritor's Powder: A Tale of Arsenic, Murder, and the New Forensic Science* (New York: W.W. Norton Co., 2014), 27.

but due in part to John Stuart Mill's intervention, that section of the bill was ultimately overturned. Shopkeepers still had to keep records of who bought arsenic, where they lived, and the purpose of the purchase.[30]

The precautions weren't entirely effective. As the *British Journal of Haematology* noted, "Such laws relating to the sale and purchase of arsenic may have contributed to fewer arsenic-related murders but they still continued, as evidenced in the late 20th century by 13 convictions of women poisoning their husbands for insurance money in Philadelphia and California."[31]

30. Judith Knelman, "The Amendment of the Sale of Arsenic Bill," *Victorian Review* 17, no. 2 (Winter 1991), https://www.jstor.org/stable/27794686?seq=1.

31. Derek Doyle, "Notoriety to Respectability: A Short History of Arsenic Prior to Its Present Day Use in Haematology," *British Journal of Haematology* 145, issue 3 (April 6, 2009), https://doi.org/10.1111/j.1365-2141.2009.07623.x.

Section 3

BAD FAM

*The family that slays together
does not stay together.*

LIZZIE BORDEN

(1860–1927)

When my husband and I started thinking about whether to have children, we talked about the worst-case scenarios. He said, "They could be very sick." I said, "They could murder us, their parents, like Lizzie Borden." I still feel my outcome is the worst, one so biblically terrible that even a hundred years later, fascination with the Borden case endures. She has inspired television shows, musicals, and even a children's rhyme. It goes:

Lizzie Borden took an ax,
and gave her mother forty whacks.

When she saw what she had done,
she gave her father forty-one.[1]

The number is inaccurate. Lizzie Borden's father received eleven whacks, and her stepmother eighteen.

That error aside, the poem does give away most of what happened.

In 1892 Lizzie Borden supposedly murdered both her parents with an ax. This was surprising not simply because of the violence of the act, but because the family was relatively well-to-do and respectable. They were regarded as mildly eccentric—her father was so thrifty that he refused to pay for running water or electricity in their house in a time when most Americans had adopted the conveniences—but in general they were thought of as very clean-cut, upstanding people. The Borden girls, Lizzie and her older sister Emma, were active with the local church and charities.

It came as a shock when, on August 4, 1892, Lizzie calmly told Bridget the family maid that she had found her father's body brutally bludgeoned to death in the home's sitting room. Her stepmother Abby's body was found in the upstairs guest room.

There was an abundance of evidence to indicate that Lizzie was the perpetrator. She was open about her hatred for her stepmother. She failed to maintain a consistent story when she was asked about her whereabouts. The week before, Mrs. Borden had consulted the family physician because, after a bout of illness, she strongly suspected someone in the house was trying to poison her. Lizzie had been seen attempting to buy the poison prussic acid the day before the murders. She was turned away from the shop, and immediately afterward her parents wound up dead. Her defenders pointed to the fact that she was not covered in blood when she reported the murder, although she was in her own house and certainly could have cleaned herself and changed before calling Bridget.

---

1. Sarah Hughes, "She Gave Her Mother 40 Whacks: The Lasting Fascination with Lizzie Borden," *The Guardian*, December 3, 2016, https://www.theguardian.com/books/2016/dec/04/lizzie-borden-40-whacks-lasting-fascination.

Meanwhile, a few days later she burnt what she claimed was a paint-stained dress, which was (and is) an odd way to dispose of dresses. A hatchet was found in the Borden basement with its handle removed, possibly to hide the fact that it was bloody.

If you are a parent, you might wonder how to avoid having this happen to you.

The best answer is to make some vague effort to get along with your kids. A few modern biographers suspect that Lizzie was abused by her parents, something that would have been covered up at the time. Some suspect that she was a victim of incest, leading to this outburst of especially violent rage.

At the very least, Lizzie was a thirty-two-year-old woman who lived with parents she did not get along with, and might have seen murder as the only way to achieve independence.

Lizzie was a classic case of someone who avoided a murder conviction because she was female and wealthy and at least *seemed* ladylike. At her preliminary trial her counsel, Andrew J. Jennings, begged the judge, "Don't put this stigma of guilt upon this woman, raised as she has been and with a past character beyond reproach." The jury seemed to agree. At trial it was repeatedly stated that a genteel woman like Lizzie—a woman who volunteered with the church!— would be incapable of any kind of murder, let alone ax murder. To the jury's eyes, she did not *look* like a murderer. Despite the evidence against Lizzie, she was not only found not guilty, but the verdict was rendered within thirty-five minutes. As she walked away, the *Boston Globe* happily reported that "Lizzie Borden was to live, to love and be loved, barring any moral accidents, for many years to come."[2]

Well, not quite.

In spite of the not guilty verdict, the stigma that Jennings predicted did live on. People might have been fine freeing her, but they didn't want to hang out with her afterward. In 1913 the *Pennsylvania Standard* reported that she lived a reclusive life with only her servants and sister for company. Even her sister moved

---

2. "Not Guilty," *The Boston Globe,* June 21, 1893.

out by 1905, claiming, someway mysteriously, "I did not go until conditions became absolutely unbearable,"[3] making Lizzie "the most isolated free woman in New England."[4] That said, she lived in a very lovely house, fully equipped with running water, and, perhaps sensibly to her mind, never had any children.

3. "Lizzie Borden's Isolated Life After Her Murder Trial," Biography.com, May 23, 2019, https://www. biography.com/news/lizzie-borden-life-after-murder-trial.

4. "Condemned by Public Opinion," *The Standard* (Lykens, PA), April 25, 1913.

LEONARDA CIANCIULLI

(1894–1970)

Being a mom is *hard*. Or, being a "good mother" is hard, especially as what that constitutes is different for all of us. Maybe you feel like you must only feed your children organic food. Or that you shouldn't allow them too much access to screens. Or, if you are Leonarda Cianciulli, that you should commit acts of human sacrifice to protect them.

See? Different for everyone.

In Leonarda's youth, a psychic prophesied that her life would be filled with unhappiness and that "you will marry and have children, but your children will die." She also claimed that "one hand tells me you will end up in prison.

The other a criminal asylum . . . it will be one or the other."[5] That psychic was correct. Over the course of her marriage, Leonarda had three miscarriages and gave birth to fourteen children, but ten of them died before reaching adulthood.

At the dawn of World War II, her eldest son, Giuseppe, joined the Italian army. Leonarda couldn't bear the thought of losing another child. Like many mothers during wartime, she was desperate for some way to protect him. Unlike many mothers, she turned to what the *Baltimore Sun* claimed was a "ceremony reminiscent of the witches of the dark ages."[6]

She believed that in order to spare her son, she could sacrifice another life. Perhaps to be on the safe side, however, she sacrificed three lives. This strikes me as somewhat overenthusiastic, but then, I have never participated in any human sacrifice ceremonies.

Leonarda's three victims—Faustina Setti, Francesca Soavi, and Virginia Cacioppo—were all struggling, emotionally or financially, and searching for new opportunities. Faustina was a lonely spinster. Francesca wanted a job. Virginia, a former opera singer, wished to return to the world of music. Leonarda summoned each separately to her house. She claimed to have found a husband for Faustina, a position teaching at a girls' school for Francesca, and work as a secretary for an impresario for Virginia. All of these opportunities just happened to be in another town, where the women were told they would have to move. She encouraged them to write postcards to their friends telling them that they were leaving. Then she offered them a drugged drink to toast their good fortune, picked up an ax, and murdered them. In at least the first case, she nearly beheaded the woman in one swoop.

It's nice to think that these women were at least happy and hopeful in their final moments, because what came after was truly gruesome.

Leonarda cut their decapitated bodies into pieces and put those parts into a pot in which soda was boiling. She found that the process produced a waxy

5. R. Barri Flowers, ed., *Masters of True Crime: Chilling Stories of Murder and the Macabre* (New York: Prometheus Books, 2012), 87.

6. "Rendered Her Friends to Wax, She Says, Gypsy Tale Fulfilled," *Baltimore Sun*, April 28, 1946.

substance that she quickly realized could be turned into candles. Upon inserting a wick, she remarked, "Greatness of God, what a superb flame!"[7]

As for the blood? She began using it as a baking ingredient in cookies. She proudly recounted her recipe, claiming, "I used to mix human blood with chocolate and add an exquisite flavor made of tangerine, aniseed vanilla and cinnamon. Sometimes I added a sprinkling of powder made from human bones."[8] Leonarda revealed that she gave them to her neighbors, but that she and her family also enjoyed the treats.

The third of her victims, Virginia Cacioppo, met an even more horrifying fate. Leonarda recalled, "Her flesh was fat and white; when it had melted I added a bottle of cologne, and after a long time on the boil I was able to make some most acceptable creamy soap. I gave bars to neighbors and acquaintances. The cakes, too, were better: that woman was really sweet."[9]

This is not the way anyone wishes to be complimented.

It was Virginia's sister who eventually urged the police to investigate Leonarda. When they did, she confessed to the crimes almost immediately, perhaps hoping that she could show a good reason for her human sacrifices. Predictably, they were less than understanding. Like everyone, they were bewildered that a popular, middle-aged lady of the town would commit such crimes. Why, they wondered, did Leonarda think these murders would protect her son?

Because, and I can't stress this enough, *she was insane*, likely deranged from grief during a time when heartbroken mothers were offered little if any psychological help.

Giuseppe did survive the war, but then he had to appear at his mother's murder trial in 1946. She appeared unbothered by her crimes, to which she quite calmly confessed.

Leonarda was sentenced to thirty years in prison and three in a criminal asylum, just as the psychic she had met in her youth had predicted. God willing, there, she did not do any of the cooking.

---

7. "Rendered Friends to Wax," *Baltimore Sun*.

8. "Rendered Friends to Wax," *Baltimore Sun*.

9. "The Correggio Soap-Maker," Museo Criminologico, September 12, 2006, https://web.archive.org/web/20060912155116/http://www.museocriminologico.it/correggio_uk.htm.

CHRISTINE PAPIN (1905–1937) & LÉA PAPIN (1911–2001)

TORTURE

If you had any *Downton Abbey* fantasies about how wonderful it would be to be tended to by loyal servants, the Papin sisters are here to murder those notions. Just as they murdered their employer.

Christine and Lea were children of a troubled marriage. They were raised in Le Mans, France, by aunts and uncles when they were young, after which they were sent to a Catholic orphanage. They remained remarkably close and were desolate when separated from one another. Once they entered the workforce, they chose to be maids for the same family so they could stay together.

By 1926 they seemed to have found tolerable employment with the Lancelin family. They earned three hundred francs a month, and from that "had managed to save up to 23,000 francs."[10] The girls were said to be excellent maids, so good that they were referred to as "the two pearls" by the Lancelin's neighbors and seen as "patterns of piety and morality."[11]

Sadly, Madame Lancelin suffered from mental illness. She began to have violent outbursts and abused the two sisters. Among other things, each day she would put on white gloves and run her hands over surfaces. If she found any dust, she would slap the sisters. Léa recalled being beaten because she spilled water on a table while watering plants.

The tension between the girls and their employers grew. In February 1933, when Christine was twenty-eight and Lea was twenty-two, the electrical power went out. The sisters explained that the outage was because Christine had plugged in a faulty iron. Madame Lancelin proceeded to attack them. In return, they gouged out Madame Lancelin's eyes, as well as those of her daughter. Then they beat their heads to pulp with a pewter pot and hacked their bodies into pieces.

They cleaned the knives but left at least one eyeball to roll about on the first-floor landing.

When Mr. Lancelin returned home, he found the door to his house locked. After knocking for a while, he called the police to help him enter. Upon breaking in, the police found blood, brains, and the aforementioned eyeball. Christine and Léa were quite calm, declaring, "We were waiting for you."[12]

Some French intellectuals, including Jean Genet and Simone de Beauvoir, felt that the Papin sisters' rapid transformation was the natural result of a bourgeois system designed to exploit women and the poor. Observing the trial, de Beauvoir speculated that "What was responsible was the orphanage into which

---

10. "Can France Go Through with the Guillotine for Its Most Brutal Murderess?" *The Semi-Weekly Spokesman Review* (Spokane, WA), December 17, 1933.

11. "After Years of Ill Treatment They Abruptly Turn On Their Mistress, Kill Her," *Pittsburgh Sun-Telegraph* (Pittsburgh, PA), January 6, 1935.

12. "Turn on Mistress, Kill Her," *Pittsburgh Sun-Telegraph*.

they had been put as children, the way they had been weaned, the whole hideous system designed by so-called 'good people' and which produces madmen, murderers and monsters. The horror of society's grinding machine could only be exposed by a corresponding, exemplary horror."[13] There was an inclination to lionize Christine and Léa and declare that they had struck a blow for oppressed classes everywhere.

But the Papin sisters did not seem to feel they were making a political statement, or at least they made no effort to argue as much in court. It is true that servants were often treated terribly, but the sisters did not appear to hate the *idea* of servitude so much as they hated their particular employer.

While the prosecution attempted to argue that they were insane, throughout much of the trial they appeared bored, or even to be dozing. One of the few moments when Léa roused was when the prosecutor accused Christine of telling Léa to tear Madame Lancelin's eyes out, saying, "Your sister obeyed, as she always has done." To that, Léa screamed, "Yes!"[14]

Acting as though she was merely the willing pupil or slave of her older sister was enough to ensure that Léa escaped the death penalty. She was sentenced to ten years in prison. Christine was perceived as the mastermind behind the crimes, and she was sentenced to death by guillotine. That sentence was eventually changed to life in imprisonment, but the sentence was irrelevant. So distraught was Christine at being kept away from her sister—the only true family and friend she had ever known—that she starved herself to death in prison.

Léa was released from prison in 1941.

She went back to work as a maid.

---

13. Helen Birch, ed., *Moving Targets: Women, Murder, and Representation* (Berkeley: University of California Press, 1994), 8.

14. "Guillotine for Brutal Murderess?" *The Semi-Weekly Spokesman Review.*

SUSAN ATKINS

(1948–2009)

Countless teenagers hate their parents and no longer want to live at home. In this regard, Susan Atkins was not unusual.

She was born to a middle-class family and seems to have had a relatively happy childhood. Like Lizzie Borden, she was active with her local church (which speaks less to the notion that "women who volunteer with the church are all murderers in waiting" than "respectable women have historically been limited in terms of permissible leisure activities"). When she was fifteen, her mother died of cancer. Just before she died, Susan wholesomely arranged for the church group to sing Christmas carols beneath her window.

That's a charming, socially acceptable activity. It was brought up a great deal at her trial, probably in part because it was one of the last charming, socially acceptable activities she engaged in.

Susan's situation deteriorated rapidly following her mother's death. Her father, who had always been a heavy drinker, left his children to look for work. They were shuttled back and forth between relatives. Susan soon dropped out of school and moved to San Francisco, where she worked as a topless dancer.

In 1967, she met Charlie Manson at a house party, where he was playing guitar. He claimed that "Susan introduced herself to me, saying how much she loved listening to my music. . . . A few minutes later we were up in her room making love. . . . When it was all over she was limp as a rag doll, whispering, 'Charlie, Charlie, Charlie, oh my God.'" She may have meant that literally, as she later likened Charles Manson to her own version of Jesus, claiming that only moments after meeting him she "went down and kissed his feet."[15]

Soon after that party she moved to southern California with him, becoming part of the Manson "Family," which included other disaffected young people like herself. They settled at the Spahn Movie Ranch, where westerns used to be filmed. Charlie renamed Susan "Sadie Mae Glutz." In 1968 she gave birth to a son who Charlie did not father, but he convinced her to name the child Zezozose Zadfrack Glutz.

I would like to say that giving a child that name is the cruelest thing Susan did, but of course it isn't.

Before long, activities at the ranch took a terrifying turn. Money was running out. The drug dealing that the members of the Manson Family were engaged in wasn't sufficiently profitable to sustain the commune. Charlie Manson had heard that a friend, Gary Hinman, had received an inheritance. He sent Susan and two other followers to steal money from him. In the process, they killed him.

This was disastrous, but then Charlie decided to start a race war, killing prominent white people and attempting to place the blame upon Black people.

---

15. Curt Gentry and Vincent Bugliosi, "The Manson Murders: A Jesus Christ Like Person to Me," *York Daily Record* (York, PA), February 4, 1975.

He was supposedly inspired by the Beatles' *White Album*, which featured a character called "Sexy Sadie" that Charlie thought was a reference to Sadie Mae Glutz, which, again, was not even Susan's real name.

The Manson Family came to believe the Beatles were communicating directly with them. Another particularly inspirational song was "Helter Skelter." This choice is quite straightforwardly about a carnival ride. It is one of the Beatles' more unobjectionable songs, far closer in its themes to "I Want to Hold Your Hand" than, for instance, "Lucy in the Sky with Diamonds." But then, white men with beards can read their own interests into pretty much any song.

So, on August 8, 1969, Susan and four other Manson devotees went to movie star Sharon Tate's home in the Hollywood Hills to murder her. According to Susan, Charlie told them to "paint a picture more gruesome than anyone had ever seen."[16] They killed five people at the house, and Sharon Tate's unborn child suffocated to death in utero. After they finished, they fixed themselves snacks and then wrote "death to all pigs," "helter skelter," and "arise" on the front door.

Remarkably, Susan might have gotten away with that crime, but when she was arrested for Hinman's death, she bragged in jail that she had murdered Sharon Tate. She even went so far as to claim that she had tasted Tate's blood and used it to write "pig" on the front door of the house.

At the Tate trial, Susan appeared girlish. Reporters noted that she described the murders "with the casualness of a child reciting what she did that day in school." The district attorney went so far as to promise her ice cream in exchange for testifying.[17] She was able to vividly describe how she murdered the victims, including how, as Sharon Tate begged for the life of her unborn child, she declared, "Woman, I have no mercy for you."[18]

---

16. Gentry and Bugliosi, "The Manson Murders."

17. Gentry and Bugliosi, "The Manson Murders."

18. "Susan Atkins Tells Jury of Murders," *The Atlanta Constitution*, February 23, 1975.

The impact was horrifying. Years later, Debra Tate, Sharon Tate's sister, would read a letter from their father recalling how "I sat in a courtroom with a jury and watched with others. I saw a young woman who giggled, snickered and shouted out insults, even while testifying about my daughter's last breath, she laughed."[19] At her sentencing she mocked the court, telling them, "You'd best lock your doors and watch your own kids."[20]

The court declined to let Susan watch hers. Her son was legally adopted in 1972.

19. Associated Press, "Susan Atkins Fails to Get Parole in Tate Killing," *Los Angeles Times*, December 29, 2000, https://www.latimes.com/archives/la-xpm-2000-dec-29-mn-5953-story.html.

20. Times Staff Reports, "Remembering Charles Manson's Victims," *Los Angeles Times*, November 20, 2017.

FEMALE CULT LEADERS

When you think of cult leaders, you likely consider a bearded man wearing a weirdly stained white robe, who looks like he reeks of patchouli and sweaty opportunism.

Well, good news fellow women! We are breaking through the glass ceiling straight to the comet-filled skies, because women can also be cult leaders. Consider these three women exemplars of horrible family dynamics.

ANNE HAMILTON-BYRNE
(1921–2019)

From the 1960s to the 1980s, Australian yoga teacher Anne Hamilton-Byrne led a cult called The Family. That's an appealing name, except many of the children in The Family were "acquired" through irregular adoptions. When the cult members were not stealing children, they were encouraged to "hand over their own children to Hamilton-Byrne and 'aunties' to be raised as part of a so-called master race."[21] They were kept in seclusion and home-schooled, subject to beatings and starvation diets, dressed alike with uniformly dyed blonde hair, and regularly given psychiatric drugs. Unsurprisingly, this cult did not become a master race, but it did cause a lot of childhood trauma.

21. Australian Associated Press, "Family Cult Leader Anne Hamilton-Byrne Dead at 98," *The Guardian*, June 14, 2019, https://www.theguardian.com/world/2019/jun/14/family-cult-leader-anne-hamilton-byrne-dead-at-98.

SILVIA MERAZ
(B. 1968)

Silvia was the leader of the cult of Santa Muerte (Saint Death),[22] a pleasant group that mostly helped the poor and gave out free hugs. Hah! No. The members of the cult of Saint Death were obviously going to kill people. Their first victim was a fifty-five-year-old woman. The next two were ten-year-old boys. Silvia and her eight followers smeared the blood of their victims on an altar in the hope that it would bring them riches. Instead, they were caught by the Mexican state police. Silvia's actions brought her a life sentence in jail.

VALENTINA DE ANDRADE
(B. 1931)

Valentina was the head of the Superior Universal Alignment cult of Brazil. She called for caution in living with children, preaching, "Watch out for children, they are unconscious instruments of the great scam called God and his evil collaborators. . . ." An alien apparently told Valentina that anyone born after 1981 was an instrument of evil, and she followed-up by encouraging her disciples to abandon those children. Not only did her followers desert them, they allegedly went so far as to kill as many as nineteen children between 1989 and 1993. The deaths might never have been detected had the nine-year-old Wandiclei Pinheiro not escaped from his captors and gone to the police.[23] While most of Valentina's followers received life sentences for their crimes, the jury found her not guilty as she did not, herself, commit the murders.[24] She's still preaching in Argentina, which is horrifying. Though to be fair, I was born in 1986, so my feelings might be biased.

---

22. "Children 'Sacrificed' to Mexico's Cult of Saint Death," The Telegraph (London), March 31, 2012, https://www.telegraph.co.uk/news/worldnews/centralamericaandthecaribbean/mexico/9177633/Children-sacrificed-to-Mexicos-cult-of-Saint-Death.html.

23. Clarissa Cole, "Move Over Manson. There's a New Cult Leader in Town," The Criminal Code (blog), November 21, 2017, https://www.thecriminalcode.com/index.php/2017/11/21/move-over-manson-theres-a-new-cult-leader-in-town/.

24. "Brazilian Court Acquits Alleged Satanic Cult Leader in Murder Trial—2003-12-06," VOA News, October 30, 2009, https://www.voanews.com/archive/brazilian-court-acquits-alleged-satanic-cult-leader-murder-trial-2003-12-06.

MARIE LAFARGE 70

MARY ELIZABETH
WILSON 74

LINDA CALVEY 77

DIVORCING 80

Section 4

BLACK WIDOWS

Please Consider Divorce
Before You Murder Your Spouse

MARIE LAFARGE

(1816–1852)

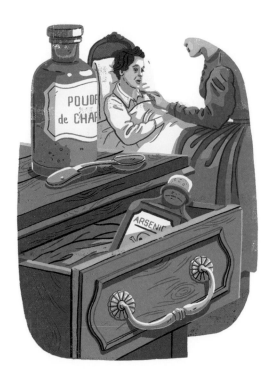

All Marie-Fortunée Capelle was supposed to do was marry well.

At first glance, that didn't seem like a terribly difficult task. She was tall and slim, with beautiful black hair and pearly white skin. She was well educated. She was said to be a descendant of King Louis XIII of France; her grandmother was the Baroness Collard. Her father was a corporal in Napoleon's army.

She had a glamorous pedigree, but money had been slowly trickling out through the generations. Both her parents died by the time she was age eighteen. That left her well-to-do aunt and uncle in charge of helping her find a suitable marriage prospect.

Along came Charles Lafarge. He was twenty-eight, so not much older than the then twenty-two-year-old Marie. He was unfortunately of lower social standing, and his attentions "were paid in a manner that shocked her refinement,"[1] but he made up for those deficits with his wealth. The *Washington Post* reported, "Lafarge's wooing lasted but five days, during which brief period he pictured the beauties of his country mansion so alluringly that he captivated the bride's heart and her imagination."[2] Marie had to be practical. She was an orphan with a limited allowance. In 1840 there were few options for making her own money. Marrying a moderately repulsive rich man, depressing as that sounds, could have been the best choice available. Like countless other women, she took the opportunity that presented itself.

The only problem was that Charles was lying. He was not nearly as wealthy as he had made himself out to be. Seemingly thinking his fortunes would improve with a wellborn wife, he enlisted people in his hometown (including the local priest) to write letters vouching for his wealth. In fact, he lived in a very ordinary, rundown house. When Marie arrived, she found that she'd be expected to share her home with a mother-in-law and a bevy of rats.

Seeing how she'd been deceived, Marie was horrified. She attempted to extricate herself from the marriage in the politest way possible, with an excuse women have used to deter men for centuries: She claimed she had another boyfriend. She wrote, "I beg your pardon on bended knee. I have wickedly deceived you. I love not you but another." It's worth noting that this was, by Marie's later admission, absolutely untrue. After attempting to clarify that it was her, not him, she offered to leave her possessions and promised she would take to the road "and live by my wits."[3]

She also claimed that if she was not freed from the marriage, she would take arsenic.

1. Sandra Hempel, *The Inheritor's Powder: A Tale of Arsenic, Murder, and the New Forensic Science* (New York: W.W. Norton Company, 2013), 198.

2. "World Famous Police Mysteries, the Case of Madame LaFarge," *Washington Post*, December 18, 1910.

3. "World Famous Police Mysteries," *Washington Post*.

Lafarge refused an annulment. And though she was clearly tempted, Marie decided not to take arsenic herself.

So Marie waited a few months. She was polite. She even seemed loving toward her husband. She encouraged him to go to Paris, writing, "Go you alone to Paris, dear Charles, and I will do everything in my power to help you by giving you introductions to old business friends of my family."[4] Before he left, she declared that she'd changed her will to ensure that he would receive her whole inheritance. Touched, he agreed to do the same.

While Lafarge was away, Marie sent him a cake, like a dutiful wife.

Upon eating it Charles became extremely ill. He imagined that the cake had merely gone bad—as you would if you didn't suspect your spouse of deliberately poisoning you—and returned to his home. And yet, once he was there, he remained ill, even as Marie stayed by his bedside. When he complained about what she was feeding him, claiming it "burned like fire,"[5] she explained it was probably because he was still drinking wine despite his illness.

Members of Charles's family became suspicious, especially since Marie had purchased arsenic from the druggist and Charles's symptoms appeared very similar to those of arsenic poisoning. His mother and sister attempted to stop Marie from nursing him and implored that he not eat or drink anything she gave him. They were unsuccessful. When they tried to share their suspicions with doctors, they were, if not outright dismissed, told there wasn't much they could do.

Charles died shortly after.

A justice of the peace was called. The stomach from Charles's body was taken for examination, and arsenic was found present.

In different circumstances, a woman might have been found guilty fairly quickly. But at the trial, Marie shone as only a woman trained from birth to be beautiful and charming could. Newspapers enthused over "the excellence of her piano playing, her delightful voice, her competence in more than one science, her reading and translation of Goethe, her fluency in several languages

---

4. "Great French Mysteries," *McClure's Magazine*, November 11, 1911.
5. "World Famous Police Mysteries," *Washington Post*.

and composing of Italian verse."[6] None of these qualities have anything to do with whether someone is a murderer, but the jurors did not seem to realize that. Marie's lawyer, Charles Lachaud, who was said to be in love with her, certainly did not. Or if he did, he was happy to overlook it.

Lachaud argued passionately that the test finding arsenic in the stomach was inconclusive. Indeed, a second test found no evidence of arsenic. Marie responded by "clasping her hands, raising her eyes to the heavens, and fainting."[7]

In light of the mixed test results, the body of Charles Lafarge had to be dug up for further tests. When the examiners prepared to exhume his body, they found it had decomposed so badly that a spoon had to be used to carefully lift portions. An expert performed the Marsh test, a toxicology exam assessing the presence of arsenic, and found Charles's remains to be riddled with it.

By that time, though only around nine months had passed, "Marie's hair was streaked with white."[8] Given her stressed appearance, the jury was, perhaps, less charmed. They took only an hour to find her guilty. She was sentenced to a life of hard labor in prison, but that sentence was quickly reduced to mere life in prison. There, she wrote her memoirs. In 1852, stricken with tuberculosis, she was released by Napoleon III and lived the rest of her brief life in Ariège. After having lived by her wits as much as a woman in the mid-1800s could, hopefully she found a house with few rats.

---

6. Hempel, *Inheritor's Powder*, 199.

7. Hempel, *Inheritor's Powder*, 199.

8. Hempel, *Inheritor's Powder*, 201.

MARY ELIZABETH WILSON

(1889–1963)

Mary Elizabeth Wilson was *fun*. She loved to laugh. She loved to screw. She liked to drink and eat and have a good time.

She also enjoyed poisoning her husbands.

Not all of them! Her marriage to her first husband lasted an admirable forty-three years. They met when Mary was working as a servant for the Knowles family. She married their son John, who worked at a shipyard. The couple had six children. But, before too long, they began to quarrel about money. Mary felt John was cramping her style, noting, "he didn't like me having a drink, and that caused rows."[9] Soon they were sleeping in separate bedrooms, much to Mary's chagrin.

To alleviate some of their financial concerns, they took in a lodger, a chimney sweep named John Russell. Before long, he and Mary became lovers. Their arrangement persisted for twenty-five years, even after John moved out (and surprisingly became very religious), though Mary continued to cook his meals and clean his house and, of course, sleep with him.

This sounds extremely time consuming for Mary and may not have been fully satisfactory to John Knowles, who passed away from tuberculosis in 1955. Despite the fact that Mary tended to him *exclusively* for the two weeks leading up to his death, he left his money to the Jarrow Gospel Hall. All Mary inherited was forty-two pounds, which she found in a cupboard. She promptly moved in with her "fancy man"[10] John Russell, but he died, debt-ridden, four months later.

If either of them had left Mary a bit more money, things might have worked out better for everyone.

As it was, Mary was forced to work as a housekeeper. She found employment with seventy-five-year-old Oliver Leonard. By most accounts, Mary was a terrible housekeeper. Oliver's house was filled with cobwebs. But she had other qualities. By September 1956, the couple married, and less than two weeks later, he was dead.

Oliver left Mary everything he had—all fifty pounds. That money lasted about a year (and I'm frankly amazed it lasted that long), at which time she answered an ad for a housekeeper placed by Ernest Wilson. Wilson claimed that he'd rather have a wife than a housekeeper, and Mary agreed, but told him she was only marrying him because she was twenty-eight dollars behind on her rent. Lest you wonder about how this sixty-two-year-old woman kept attracting suitors, she rather cavalierly quipped, "The men like Mary and I like men."[11]

She also liked killing them. Indeed, by her fourth marriage, Mary seemed to find the idea of killing people positively hilarious. At her wedding, a friend

9. Ruth Reynolds, "The Merry Widow of Windy Nook Went to Trial for Murder," *Chicago Tribune*, August 31, 1958.
10. Reynolds, "Merry Widow."
11. Reynolds, "Merry Widow."

asked Mary what she would do with the leftover sandwiches and cakes. "Keep them for the funeral," she replied.[12] Ernest laughed along with everyone else. Fifteen days later, he was dead.

At the registrar's office, where she signed both wedding and funeral certificates, Mary quipped that she was in the office so often, "There should be a discount for me."[13]

At Ernest's autopsy, phosphorus and bran—two ingredients often found in a poison used to kill roaches—were found in his viscera. Upon this realization, people noticed that the symptoms of Leonard Oliver's brief illness had been *very similar* to Ernest Wilson's.

When the police exhumed the bodies, Mary seemed unperturbed, claiming, "I gave them nothing but kindness."[14] Kindness and poison.

Her lawyer made a fairly effective case that Wilson and Oliver might have been taking phosphorus as an aphrodisiac to spice up their marriages. But that was ultimately dismissed when it became clear that the men would have to have taken 150 aphrodisiac pills to poison themselves—an unlikely error, even if they were very desperate to keep up with Mary.

The prosecutor declared that it was in fact a very simple case of "a wicked woman who married in succession two men and then deliberately poisoned them in order to get the paltry benefit which she hoped she might obtain by their deaths."[15]

It's surprising that Mary didn't benefit more financially. But then, had she not been stopped, who knows how many more times she would have been willing to repeat this pattern? A hundred dollars or so every two weeks would add up.

She was sentenced to death, but ultimately given a reprieve to life imprisonment. But then, for a woman with such a zeal for life—and male company—living out the remainder of her days in a women's prison may have been a fate worse than death.

---

12. "Jokes Prove Dangerous," *The Province* (Vancouver, BC), April 5, 1958.
13. "Jokes Prove Dangerous," *The Province*.
14. "Windy Nook Widow Suspect," *Pawhuska Journal-Capital* (Pawhuska, OK), December 12, 1957.
15. Reynolds, "Merry Widow."

LINDA CALVEY
(1948–PRESENT)

RAPE

Women's magazines are constantly offering up lists of things men don't like women doing. You may be relieved to know that killing men really doesn't appear to be a turn-off. Just look at the luck Linda Calvey had in love despite, as one police officer noted, everyone she was with ending up dead or imprisoned.

Linda came from a middle-class family in East London. She had lofty goals, telling her relatives at age twelve, "One day I'm going to have a red Rolls Royce and a fur coat."[16]

---

16. Duncan Campbell, "From Professional Armed Robber to the 'Black Widow': The Story of Linda Calvey," *The Byline Times*, August 27, 2019, https://bylinetimes.com/2019/08/27/from-professional -armed-robber-to-the-black-widow-the-story-of-linda-calvey/.

At nineteen she fell in love with Mickey Calvey, who was what some would think of as "bad news" and what others would consider "an honest to goodness bank robber."

"I married a bank robber when I was 22 because I fell in love with him," Linda claimed. "I knew Mickey Calvey was a bank robber the day I met him at his homecoming party after his release from prison. I went into it with my eyes open."[17] Indeed, she seemed to embrace their life in crime, helping Mickey as a getaway driver and later wielding a gun alongside him.

But then Mickey was gunned down in 1978.

Despite earning a million pounds through robberies, after Mickey's death, Linda had financial concerns. Those were alleviated somewhat by her lover Ronnie Cook. Grim and controlling, Ronnie wasn't as much fun as Mickey. Linda later told a reporter, "Mickey was flamboyant, [an] extrovert, smart, the man about town. Ronnie was quiet, soberly dressed. He had a reputation as a hard man and nobody messed with him."[18] That did not equate to him being an especially nice partner.

Linda may not have mourned when Ronnie was imprisoned in 1981 for an eight-hundred-pound security van robbery. Even in prison he remained controlling, dictating the sexy outfits she was supposed to wear when visiting, one of which was lingerie under her fur coat (so, she did get that fur coat after all). She agreed, but only because she thought, "with any luck I'll give him a heart attack."[19]

It did not work. Given what happened next, he may have wished it had.

In 1990, Ronnie was released from prison. By then, Linda had a new lover, "another prisoner, a strong, good-looking bloke."[20] His name was Danny

17. Mike Brooke, "'Black Widow' Robber Linda Calvey Tells Why She Couldn't Have Shot Dead Brink's-Mat Raider Ron Cook," *The Docklands and East London Advertiser*, July 6, 2019, https://www. eastlondonadvertiser.co.uk/news/heritage/black-widow-book-launch-by-author-linda-calvey-1-6145768.

18. Kate Kray, *Killers: Britain's Deadliest Murderers Tell Their Stories* (London: King's Road Publishing, 2014), 108.

19. Brooke, "'Black Widow' Robber Linda Calvey."

20. Kate Kray, "Natural Born Killers," adapted by Mike Ridley, The Free Library, 2000, https://www. thefreelibrary.com/.

Reece. The couple, probably correctly, felt that Ronnie would not look favorably upon their romance. Linda supposedly offered Danny £10,000 to murder Ronnie. Danny was, at least in theory, up for it. However, he panicked at the last moment. He claimed, "I aimed the gun but at the last moment I shot to the side, hitting him in the elbow. He fell backwards. I aimed my gun again but froze. I'd never killed anyone." Undeterred, he said that at that point "[Linda] screamed 'Kneel,' then pointed the gun and shot Ronnie in the head."[21]

Linda denied this account for the rest of her life, but she was sentenced to eighteen years' imprisonment. This didn't seem to dim Danny Reece's ardor, nor Linda's, who said, "When I was found guilty, I held Danny's hand tight as they led us down to the cells. They took Danny one way, me the other."[22] The couple married while Linda was in prison, but the marriage ended in divorce. Reece was later accused of raping another prison inmate in 2011.

Upon her release, she found love yet again. Her third husband, George Caesar, wasn't involved in crime but didn't seem perturbed by her reputation. When a reporter asked if he'd at least considered a prenup before they wed in 2008, he replied, "You can't go into a marriage thinking like that. You have to trust people. Life's a gamble, but if you lose trust, what have you got? So, she might kill me. Well, hell, I'll take the chance."[23]

George has since passed away, as far as we know from natural causes, not Linda's hand.

---

21. Kray, "Natural Born Killers."

22. Kray, "Natural Born Killers."

23. Jenny Johnston, "Would You Marry the Black Widow? Ex-gangster Linda Calvey Finds a New Fiancé," *Daily Mail*, December 18, 2008, https://www.dailymail.co.uk/femail/article-1097064/Would -marry-black-widow-Ex-gangster-Linda-Calvey-finds-new-fiance.html.

DIVORCING

Don't listen to people who bemoan the modern divorce rate. Yes, a marriage falling apart is sad for everyone involved. However, the fact that divorce is now relatively easy to obtain is positive. Because when two people are forced to miserably stay together, the situation is generally disastrous, if not outright deadly.

The religious rules that kept King Henry VIII of England from divorcing his first wife, Catherine of Aragon, and marrying Anne Boleyn meant that he broke away from the Catholic Church to form the Church of England. This led to persecution of Catholics (and then Protestants) for decades to come. And the ability to divorce did not improve. In England, divorce was nearly impossible to obtain prior to the 1857 Matrimonial Causes Act. It was so prohibitively expensive that only about ten divorces were granted each year.[24]

A woman was trapped. As the Honorable Mrs. Norton wrote in 1855, "An English wife may not leave her husband's house. Not only can he sue her for 'restitution of conjugal rights,' but he has a right to enter the house of any friend or relation with whom she may take refuge, and who may 'harbour her,'—as it is termed—and carry her away by force, with or without the aid of the police."[25]

In Charles Dickens's *Hard Times*, published in 1854, one of the characters bemoans how much he wishes to escape his miserable marriage. He goes to a friend to ask if there is any way that he might obtain a divorce, especially as he has read, "th' supposed unpossibility o' ever getting unchained from one another, at any price, on any terms, brings blood upon this land, and brings many common married fok to battle, murder, and sudden death." The brunt

24. Margaret Wood, "Marriage and Divorce 19th Century Style," *In Custodia Legis* (blog), Library of Congress, February 23, 2018, https://blogs.loc.gov/law/2018/02/marriage-and-divorce-19th-century-style/.

25. Caroline Elizabeth Sarah Norton, *A Letter to the Queen on Lord Chancellor Cranworth's Marriage and Divorce Bill* (London: Longman, Brown, Green and Longmans, 1855), http://digital.library.upenn.edu/women/norton/alttq/alttq.html.

of that abuse fell on women. In 1828, after the Offences Against the Person Act was passed in Britain, "the magistrates courts were flooded with abused wives."[26]

When there is no way out of an abusive or miserable situation, some will turn to murder. And considering that outcome, modern-day fighting over who keeps the wedding china is highly preferable.

26. Jennifer Komorowski, "Exposing the Monsters Behind Victorian Domestic Abuse" (undergraduate awards paper, Western University, 2014), https://ir.lib.uwo.ca/cgi/viewcontent.cgi?article=1007&context= ungradawards_2014.

Section 5

SCORNED WOMEN

Hell hath no fury.

DARYA SALTYKOVA

(1730–1801)

What does it mean to handle a break-up well? To wish your ex a loving good-bye and best of luck on all their future endeavors? Not many people manage that level of civility. It's almost impossible to pretend a break-up isn't personal, when it is one of the *most* personal things someone can experience. It's not surprising people don't behave well.

It's a relief, though, that most do not behave like Darya Saltykova.

Darya was born with what appeared to be every blessing in mid-eighteenth-century Russia. She came from a wealthy family and was married to an even wealthier man. Darya was twenty-five years old when he died, and suddenly she was the mistress of large Russian estates and the owner of hundreds of serfs.

Having slaves, *sorry*, serfs, is quite bad in whatever period you live in—at least for the serfs.

However, to be a young widow was a fate dearly hoped for by many wealthy women in history. It meant financial independence and the ensuing freedom to have romantic affairs and to choose your next husband for love.

Darya embraced this autonomy. During her marriage she'd been known as a pious and introverted woman. In her widowhood, she changed. She embarked on a romance with an extremely handsome man named Nikolay Tyutchev.

For everyone's sake, it's a pity it did not go well.

The affair lasted until Darya was thirty-two. When it ended, she found out that her lover intended to marry another, younger woman. Darya became apoplectic with rage. She quite literally decided to blow the couple up, buying gunpowder and sending her serfs to the new woman's house. The serfs chose not to act—most likely since an explosion was an insane thing to do—so Darya asked them to beat the couple to death. Realizing that was no *less* insane, they informed Nikolay of Darya's intentions. He filed a report with the police, which Darya adamantly denied. And he and his new bride fled.

He had recourse. Her serfs were not so lucky.

Darya had always been a harsh mistress, even by the standards of her time. According to Tori Telfer, the author of *Lady Killers*, "Darya lit one woman's hair on fire, and pushed an 11-year-old down a stone staircase. . . . She would grab logs of wood—tucked in every room and meant for fireplaces—and use them as makeshift clubs." When her serfs escaped and attempted to report her to the authorities, she replied, laughing, "No matter how much you report or complain about me, the authorities will not do anything to me."[1] Her horrible abuses escalated after the breakdown of her love affair, but then, her abuses were always horrible. Even before her romance, her serfs were beaten to death, tied

---

1. Tori Telfer, *Lady Killers: Deadly Women Throughout History* (New York: Harper Perennial, 2017), 174.

outside, and left to starve, often because they failed to clean the house to Darya's satisfaction.

Of her 600 serfs, she murdered 138 of them.[2]

Darya's crimes were brought to the attention of Empress Catherine the Great in 1762 by two of her serfs, Yermolay Ilyin and Savely Martynov. The two had escaped from the estate after Darya killed their wives. They made their way to Moscow illegally; if they were caught, Darya would have killed them without hesitation. Against some astonishingly unlikely odds, they managed to get a letter detailing their mistress's abuses to the Empress. They begged her "to protect them from mortal ruin and merciless inhuman torment."[3]

Catherine was eager to be seen as a progressive empress. She didn't automatically dismiss the serfs' complaints as her predecessors might have. Instead, an investigator named Stephen Volkov was appointed to look into the case. Coming from a poor family, Stephen might have felt more sympathy for the serfs than the aristocracy. Certainly, he found enough evidence of Saltykova's crimes to have her tried.

Tried and, remarkably, given her aristocratic connections, found guilty.

Though the death penalty had been revoked, Darya was made to wear a sign around her neck in the public square declaring, "This woman has tortured and murdered."[4] Although, at a time when cruelty toward serfs was so prevalent, that may well have been met with a shrug by many in Darya's aristocratic class.

Darya was then sent to live in a convent basement, where she spent the rest of her days in isolation. Members of the upper classes periodically stopped by to stare at her and mock her through the bars of the cell. While her life was surely torturous, it was still more pleasant than the torments she inflicted on her serfs.

Her crimes were so notorious in Russian memory that Tolstoy addressed them while discussing his book *War and Peace*, claiming, "I know what the characteristics of the period are that people do not find in my novel—the horrors of

---

2. "Saltychikha (Saltykova Daria Nikolaeva)," History of Russia, World History, accessed January 16, 2021, http://www.istorya.ru/person/saltychiha.php.

3. "Saltychikha," History of Russia.

4. Vera Yurchenko, "Memorial," *Montgomery Advertiser* (Montgomery, AL), June 22, 2018.

serfdom, the immuring of wives, the flogging of grown-up sons, Saltykova, and so on."[5]

So, if you wonder why the people of Russia rose up against the rich, just look to Darya Saltykova.

---

5. Leo Tolstoy, *War and Peace* (Oxford: Oxford University Press, 2010), 1309.

LAURA FAIR
(1837–1919)

There are many somewhat antiquated sayings advising young women to be wary of men's promises. There are fewer advising young men against breaking those promises. People imagine that women won't shoot lying men. They've forgotten about Laura Fair.

Laura had a troubled life long before she murdered anyone. She was born into poverty in Alabama in 1837. By the time she was age sixteen, her family had settled in New Orleans, where she found a wealthy husband. According to the *Elk County Advocate*, "She was eighteen and he was eighty. His senile jealousy soon drove her to the remedy of divorce."[6] Conveniently he died before the divorce could be finalized.

Laura was free to marry again, and she did. Unfortunately, that marriage proved unhappy as well. Her second husband was extremely abusive. How abusive? Well, he was given to shooting his pistol above her head when he was drunk. As Laura understandably did not wish to die in a game of William Tell, she filed for divorce and moved to California. There, in 1859, she met the man who would be her third husband, William Fair. He was a thirty-seven-year-old West Point graduate and respectable lawyer. Laura had every reason to think that she had finally found a stable man of a reasonable age with whom to settle down.

That thought was fleeting. William Fair was a con artist who had faked his military training. Soon after their marriage he either committed suicide or was shot by a business partner (the two were alone in a room, and all that is known for sure is that William Fair was shot). He left her with a daughter, Lillias, and debts.

A widow again at age twenty-five, she moved to Virginia City, Nevada, to open a boarding house. She was very competent, and the business was going well. Finally, life seemed to be turning around for Laura and her daughter! And there ends her story, just some romantic setbacks followed by a life as a sensible businesswoman living a nice life.

No. Of course not.

Then she met Alexander Parker Crittenden.

A forty-seven-year-old lawyer, Alexander initially told Laura he was a widower. Perhaps that gave the two something to bond over, as Laura would have been very familiar with the pain (or at least surprise) that comes with losing a spouse. Except in Alexander's case, his wife Clara was very much alive, as were eight of his children.

When Laura learned of his deception, Crittenden promised he would get a divorce—in six months, at the most.

This is a line that has been fed to women in relationships with married men for all of history.

---

6. "The Story of Laura Fair," *The Elk County Advocate* (Ridgway, PA), May 25, 1871, https://chroniclingamerica.loc.gov/lccn/sn84026259/1871-05-25/ed-1/seq-4/.

Seven years later, it was clear to Laura that Alexander had no real intention of leaving his wife. By then, she was suicidal, and was taking large amounts of sedatives. She briefly married again, to a man named Jesse Snyder, but within three months that marriage ended. Crittenden helped arrange for her divorce, but he continued to show no interest in getting one himself.

So, Laura shot him.

After another of their ongoing disagreements about whether he would get a divorce, Crittenden reunited with his wife and son who had been away on a vacation. He met them on the El Capitan ferry to San Francisco. Laura had also gone aboard. Crittenden's son, Parker, claimed he had "noticed a woman in black, heavily veiled, who seemed to be watching their actions closely."[7] She proceeded to shoot Alexander.

Laura was promptly disarmed and arrested. Crittenden died not long after, and Laura went on trial.

While she claimed to have been suffering from temporary insanity, the prosecutors attempted to paint Laura as a sex-crazed harlot who knowingly and wantonly led men to ruin. One claimed, "Her power was that of a female Hercules transcending the power of all the men of the world."[8] She was found guilty on June 3, 1871, and sentenced to hang—perhaps understandably, having shot someone in front of many witnesses.

However, women's rights advocates were quite firmly on Laura's side. They saw Crittenden as a seducer who had driven her to madness through his lies and refusal to marry her. Susan B. Anthony declared, "If all men protected all women as they would have their own wives and daughters protected, you would have no Laura Fair in your jail."[9] The journalist Jane Swisshelm declared in the *New York Tribune* that "if all such men were shot tomorrow . . . the world would sustain no loss."[10]

7. Thomas S. Duke, *Celebrated Criminal Cases of America* (San Francisco: James H. Barry Company, 1910), 67.

8. Gary Kamiya, "The Case of Laura Fair, San Francisco 1870," SFGate, June 28, 2014, https://www.sfgate.com/crime/article/The-case-of-Laura-Fair-San-Francisco-1870-5585715.php.

9. Marion S. Goldman, *Gold Diggers & Silver Miners: Prostitution and Social Life on the Comstock Lode* (Ann Arbor: University of Michigan Press, 1981), 86.

10. Carole Haber, *The Trials of Laura Fair: Sex, Murder, and Insanity in the Victorian West* (Chapel Hill: University of North Carolina Press, 2013), loc. 210 of 310, Kindle.

A reminder: This man was shot in front of his wife and young child. (A bad thing!)

While it's great to see women supporting their own, this is an extremely hot take, even by modern standards. It does, however, say something about the state of women in the world in the 1800s that prominent newspapers were so quick to jump to "kill every man who has an affair."

Laura was granted a stay of execution and, eventually, a new trial. That one had a far better outcome for Laura. At the not guilty verdict, "Some of the women cried with joy. Handkerchiefs were waved and hats were thrown up. Large number of spectators rushed to Miss Harris to congratulate her on her acquittal."[11]

Following her trial, Laura embarked on a lecture tour where she discussed the necessity of murdering the man who had sullied her honor. People did not love this take as much as those attending her trial, and angry mobs were known to gather outside the halls where she spoke.

Reports about what happened to her later are numerous. According to the *Los Angeles Times*, Laura "established a little home and supported herself [by] singing in mining camp dance halls."[12] Other reports claim that "for many years after her acquittal, Mrs. Fair made a living as a book agent in San Francisco."[13] Laura continued to insist that she was simply a respectable widow and mother, whose trust had been cruelly abused.

Despite her best efforts, if Laura Fair is remembered for anything today, it's as a grim warning to men. Don't lie to women. Especially not for a full seven years.

---

11. Haber, *Trials of Laura Fair*, loc. 210.

12. "Daughter of Noted Beauty," *Los Angeles Times*, February 7, 1913.

13. Duke, *Celebrated Criminal Cases*, 67.

MARIA BARBELLA

(1868–AFTER 1902)

RAPE

When women discuss the prevalence of sexual assault, there is always a certain person, usually a man, who suggests women should respond with physical violence. They *really* think the problem can be solved by women taking self-defense classes or going about armed to the teeth. The notion that you could be suddenly assaulted and immediately effectively respond with physical violence is generally far-fetched. Men tend to be stronger than women, and even in less violent circumstances, responding to your boss's creepy request to give you a backrub by punching him square in the jaw would probably result in your firing.

Still, there are some women who take justice into their own hands. Maria Barbella was one.

Maria was an Italian immigrant. Her family moved from the small town of Ferrandina (in the south of Italy) to New York City in 1892, where Maria found work as a seamstress. At the age of twenty-five, she had the bad fortune to meet a shoeshine man named Domenico Cataldo who was from the same area of Italy. He became enamored with Maria and began walking her home from work. Despite her family's disapproval, he claimed he wanted to marry her.

One night she let him buy her what he said was a soda. The drink was drugged. When she was barely conscious, Domenico took her up to a room in a boarding house and raped her. When she woke, he congratulated her on having been a virgin until he raped her.

Horribly, for a woman in Maria's situation, the only "respectable" option was to marry her rapist. She proceeded to ask Domenico to marry her. Indeed, her whole family begged this objectively horrible man that they had disliked until very recently to marry their daughter.

Domenico had a different idea. He claimed, "I'll find you a young man willing to marry you. I'll tell him you're a widow. I'll buy you a black dress. You'll marry him because I want you to. Then I'll come to visit you while he's at work."[14]

Gross.

Domenico was seemingly under the extremely incorrect impression that Maria enjoyed being raped by him and wanted to continue the experience. He had no intention of marrying her and taunted that he wouldn't marry someone who looked like a monkey. When Maria confronted him at a bar where he was playing cards drinking with a group of his friends, derisive as always, he shouted, "Only a pig would marry you!"

She promptly slit his throat with a straight razor, right there in the bar.

At the trial Maria explained, "I did not know what I did. I was crazy with anger because he would not marry me."[15]

14. "Murder in Little Italy," *Murder by Gaslight* (blog), October 7, 2010, http://www.murderbygaslight.com/2010/10/murder-in-little-italy.html.

15. Maria Boysun, "A Woman Scorned," *Daily News*, August 17, 2003.

An aside: In the course of writing this book, I have spent a lot of time thinking of good and bad reasons to murder someone. I'm hard pressed to think of anyone more justified than a woman who killed her rapist after he persisted in humiliating her.

So, I'm sad to say, it took only forty-five minutes for the jury to find Maria guilty. She was one of the first women sentenced to the electric chair.

Juries responded to average-looking immigrant women *very* differently than they did to pretty well off, native born-murderesses.

When she arrived at Sing Sing Prison, she was surprised to find that her cell was much more spacious than the tenement to which she was accustomed.[16] She formed a very close friendship with the warden's wife, Mrs. Sage. She learned English and had time to read.

Prominent feminists like Elizabeth Cady Stanton and the American-born Italian Countess di Brazza campaigned for a retrial.[17] Maria was eventually given one and was found not guilty.

Yet, when informed that the verdict had been overturned, newspapers reported that Maria "does not want to go, as she does not want to leave Mrs. Sage."[18] (Tenements, in case you were wondering, were very, very bad, like worse than Sing Sing bad.)

After her release, Maria returned to her old life. She worked as a seamstress. She married a man named Francisco Bruno in 1897. I wish that this had been a source of happiness, but as she told the *New York Times,* "My mother's family knew Mr. Bruno's family in Italy. I never saw him until Tuesday and I did not want to marry him. . . . My mother said I must marry him."[19]

And so, Maria exited one prison only to enter another. I can only hope that she managed to find some happiness in its confines.

---

16. Gail Collins, "An American Tragedy," *New York Times*, February 25, 1991, https://www.nytimes.com/1996/02/25/books/an-american-tragedy.html.

17. Collins, "American Tragedy."

18. "Maria Is Told the News," *New York Times*, April 22, 1896.

19. "Maria Barbella Married," *New York Times,* November 4, 1897.

BREAKING UP

Breaking up is, as the song says, hard to do. Not only are there practical logistical changes in your life, but the event can wreak havoc upon your mental state.

Studies have found that people falling in love experience brain chemistry similar to those using cocaine. New love increases the brain's levels of "feel good" chemicals like serotonin, norepinephrine, and dopamine. Love is addictive. And that's fabulous, if you stay in love forever.

However, people break up. And when that happens it is like withdrawal from cocaine.[20] A 2016 study by Case Western Reserve University showed pictures of ex-partners to people who had recently experienced an unwanted break-up. If this sounds like torture, it was. The parts of their brain that lit up looking at those pictures during fMRI scans were the same ones that light up when experiencing physical pain.[21]

The scorned may resort to desperate measures to get access to their "love drug" again—like calling their exes in the middle of the night begging to be taken back. Or, in *very* extreme cases, murdering their ex-lover's new partner.

Psychologists suggest that while you can't get over the pain of a break-up on command, you can at least distract yourself. You can find other activities that will trigger pleasure centers in your brain. You can commiserate with like-minded people. You can avoid your ex for the foreseeable future—and that includes ignoring their pictures on social media.[22]

Try to refrain from murderous plans. Otherwise, you won't just be a prisoner of love, but an actual prisoner, in a jail cell.

---

20. Berit Brogaard, "Love Is Like Cocaine: The Remarkable, Terrifying Neuroscience of Romance," *Salon*, February 14, 2015, https://www.salon.com/2015/02/14/love_is_like_cocaine_the _remarkable_terrifying_neuroscience_of_romance/.

21. Melanie Greenberg, "This Is Your Brain on a Breakup," *Psychology Today*, March 29, 2016, https://www. psychologytoday.com/us/blog/the-mindful-self-express/201603/is-your-brain-breakup.

22. Guy Winch, "To Get Over Heartbreak, First Understand That You're Experiencing Withdrawal," *Fatherly*, January 29, 2018, https://www.fatherly.com/love-money/how-to-fix-a -broken-heart-science/.

MURDEROUS
MERCENARIES

Cash ruled everything around them.

GRACE O'MALLEY

(1530–1603)

Pirates don't care as much about gender as they do whether people are willing to plunder and kill. And for a while, Grace O'Malley was their queen.

Grace O'Malley is a modern English approximation of her name. In Irish it was Gráinne Ní Mháille. She was born into a clan known for its seafaring skills. Fourteenth-century bards used to sing, "A good man never was there of the O'Malleys but a mariner."[1] From an early age, Grace loved the sea. She chopped off her hair to accompany her father on voyages disguised as a boy. It didn't fool anyone, but it did result in the nickname "Bald Grace."

---

1. Vance Wynn, "Weekly True Story—Grace O'Malley, the Irish Pirate," *Pittsburgh Press* (Pittsburgh, PA), May 3, 1931.

When Grace was only nineteen years old, her father died. He left his fleet of vessels to her.

Grace put them to effective use.

By this time, Grace was married to a chieftain named Donal O'Flaherty. His family was so warlike and combative that the O'Flahertys were forbidden from entering the city of Galway. Indeed, over the city's gate was posted a sign that declared, "From the ferocious O'Flahertys, Good Lord Deliver Us."[2] Grace stationed her ships in the Galway harbor and began charging people looking to enter the city for "safe passage." If they didn't pay, Grace and her fellow sailors robbed them. It is a total mob-boss move, and it worked—at least until the people of Galway attacked her castle, where she lived when she was not on board her ship. She ordered the roof of the castle stripped off, melted down, and poured on top of them. People began to say that Grace had "overstepped the bounds of womanhood,"[3] but I'm pretty sure Grace didn't care, because she was already busy stealing from or killing people who said things like that.

Following her husband's death, she amassed a pirate army of more than two hundred men. By 1566, she married again but didn't forsake any of her war-like or seafaring ways. The marriage only lasted about a year. The marriage contract had stipulated that either of the couple could end it after a year by saying "I dismiss you."[4] Grace said it almost immediately. Perhaps, like many seafaring folk of legend, she considered herself married to the sea.

One of the more famous tales about her comes from that marriage and involves her giving birth to her son Tiobóid. She was on board her ship, and while she was in labor, Algerians attacked. She rose from her bed scarcely an hour after giving birth, her newborn in her arms, to defeat them and seize their ship.[5]

---

2. Anne Chambers, *Pirate Queen of Ireland: The Adventures of Grace O'Malley* (West Link Park, Cork, Ireland: The Collins Press, 2006), loc. 250 of 1132, Kindle.

3. Chambers, *Pirate Queen*, loc. 295.

4. William E. Curtis, "Kingdom of Grace O'Malley," *Evening Star* (Washington, DC), August 26, 1908.

5. "Grace O'Malley, Irish Female Pirate," Royal Museums Greenwich, https://www.rmg.co.uk/discover/explore/graceomalley.

English officials began to write to Queen Elizabeth I, informing her that Grace was "a terror to all merchantmen who sailed the Atlantic."[6] Which is to say, she was very good at her job. In 1586 she was captured by the English and imprisoned in Dublin Castle. She was there for eighteen months before regaining her freedom. How she managed that is unclear, but I like to think that maybe Queen Elizabeth I appreciated seeing another woman overstepping a few bounds.

The two women who refused to be mastered wouldn't meet until 1593, when Grace's sons were captured by Sir Richard Bingham. Grace met with the queen and agreed to stop attacking the Crown provided her sons were returned and Richard Bingham was fired.

Both kept their promises.

For a very brief while.

At the meeting, Queen Elizabeth supposedly offered to make Grace a countess. Grace declined. She explained that "she, too, was a Queen."[7]

And who are we to say she was wrong?

---

6. Wynn, "Weekly True Story."

7. Richard M. O'Hanrahan, "A World Apart, Tory Island," *Baltimore Sun*, March 14, 1937.

KATHERINE FERRERS

(1634–1660)

If you've seen the movie *The Favourite*, you already know that life as a seventeenth-century noblewoman was full of pitfalls and vaguely terrifying. It was the woman's responsibility to run the household, manage the servants, and raise the children. She might be involved in the running of her family's or her husband's estates and businesses, but she had very few rights. She could not vote, own land, or even report domestic abuse. There was no financial security. And the weight of social implications on her reputation was heavy.

So, who could blame Lady Katherine Ferrers for becoming so fed up with the restrictions placed upon her that she became a highwaywoman? Well, other than officers of the law.

Katherine was married at age fourteen to young Thomas Fanshawe. He was, according to Samuel Pepys, "a rascally fellow, without a penny in his purse."[8] In true rascally fashion, after the wedding he promptly disappeared with most of Katherine's inheritance. Her family had died, and Katherine was left largely to her own devices, though with a country house and some servants. She was bored, lonely, and by all accounts something of a recluse.

A few years later, she met Ralph Chaplin, a neighboring farmer—during the day. At nightfall he rode out robbing people. Katherine appreciated his bad boy streak, and she certainly could have used some extra money. Before long, she joined his nighttime horseback rides, like a seventeenth-century version of Bonnie and Clyde. (Fun fact: Faye Dunaway, of *Bonnie and Clyde* movie fame, also starred in *The Wicked Lady,* a movie about Katherine Ferrers made in 1983.)

Now, legends about Katherine are inconsistent and have almost certainly grown in the telling. But the tales are also too irresistible not to share.

This was a period rife with crime. Women seemed perfectly capable of commanding armies of seafaring pirates, so it doesn't seem far-fetched that a wellborn but cash poor woman might take to a land-based kind of piracy. And if being a highwaywoman sounds morally wrong, it also sounds really liberating. She wore a costume! Perhaps more importantly: She terrorized the men who had historically exerted control over every aspect of her existence! Katherine was not the first eighteen-year-old to partake in some ill-advised actions for kicks.

Katherine would wait in trees to drop down in front of oncoming coaches, her pistol drawn, demanding the passengers' money. Unlike other highwaymen who were loath to resort to violence and were known to charm some of the people they robbed, Katherine and Ralph had no hesitation about shooting

---

8. Samuel Pepys, *The Diary of Samuel Pepys*, edited with additions by Henry B. Wheatley F.S.A. (London: George Bell & Sons), 53.

their victims.[9] Their frightening partnership didn't last long. Chaplin was executed after robbing on the highway of Finchley Common.

But Chaplin's death didn't deter Katherine, whose bloodlust only seemed to increase. She is said to have had a secret room in Markyate Cell, her manor house, where she changed into her nighttime disguise. That sounds like sexy and fabulous superhero behavior, but Katherine's actions veered more toward villainy. Stories began of a "wicked lady" clad in "a three-cornered hat, a black mask, black riding cloak and scarf, and breeches, riding a black horse with white flashes on its forelegs."[10] It's said that she shot a policeman on his own doorstep. She was also reported to have slaughtered cattle and burned down homes as families slept.[11]

Her reign of terror came to an end when she attempted to rob a wagon near Gustard Wood. She shot the driver but failed to notice there was a passenger on board. He shot her. Katherine did not die immediately and rode back toward her home. There, the *Steeple Times* noted, "She is said to have been discovered wearing men's clothing by her servants and allegedly haunts the house and surrounding area to this day."[12]

People who have walked in the vicinity of her home claim to have seen a figure wearing a three-cornered hat who disappears into the mist almost immediately. If Katherine is a ghost, she can't be more frightening in her current form than she was in life. But if you pass by Markyate Cell, you might want to keep a few coins in your pocket. Just in case.

---

9. Fiona McDonald, *Gentlemen Rogues & Wicked Ladies: A Guide to British Highwaymen & Highwaywomen* (Cheltenham, UK: The History Press, 2011), loc. 1614 of 2649, Kindle.

10. "Katherine Ferrers—the Wicked Lady," *Crime Library* (blog), *Watford Observer* (Watford, UK), https://www.watfordobserver.co.uk/news/nostalgia/crimelibrary/katherineferrers/.

11. McDonald, *Gentlemen Rogues*, loc. 1614.

12. Matthew Steeples, "The Wicked Lady," *Steeple Times*, November 11, 2013, https://thesteepletimes.com/opulence-splendour/wicked-lady/.

CHING SHIH
(1775–1844)

RAPE + TORTURE

Ching Shih was certainly not likely to become a wealthy woman based upon her background. That did not stop her.

In her early years, Ching was a prostitute. It's unlikely that she enjoyed this kind of work, but she was *good* at it. She became adept at coaxing secrets from her clients to use as leverage later.[13] She caught the eye of Cheng I, the leader of a vast pirate army known as the Red Flag. He ordered his men to steal

---

13. Urvija Banerji, "The Chinese Female Pirate Who Commanded 80,000 Outlaws," Atlas Obscura (website), April 6, 2016, https://www.atlasobscura.com/articles/the-chinese-female-pirate-who -commanded-80000-outlaws.

her from the brothel and took her as his bride, attracted by either her charms or her wily willingness to engage in underhanded behavior like blackmail.

Ching Shih may not have appreciated being forcibly kidnapped, but once again, she excelled in her circumstances. She demanded "true equality" in her marriage, meaning that half of all the profits from his fleet would go to her.[14] Within a few years the fleet had grown from two hundred ships to six hundred ships. While they had begun with the Red Fleet, they amassed so many new ships that they began to form other coalitions, known as the Yellow, Black, Blue, White, and Green fleets.

Six years after their marriage, Cheng I died. Had Ching Shih been a less formidable woman, this might have been the end of her time as a pirate as well.

Cheung Po Tsai, Cheng I's adopted son and lover (because those "adoptions" are what happens when gay marriage is not allowed), was the presumptive heir.[15] Ching Shih was not deterred. She simply took Cheung as *her* lover (and eventual husband) and seized power over the fleet.

After Cheng I's death the ship captains began to scatter. When she took power Ching scoffed, "Under the leadership of a man you have all chosen to flee. We shall see how you prove yourselves under the hand of a woman."[16]

Her ships, her rules. Some included:

• *No pirate could go ashore without permission. Punishment for a first offense was perforation of the ears; a repetition called for death.*

• *All plundered goods had to be registered before distribution. The ship responsible for the taking of a specific piece of booty received a fifth of its value; the remainder became part of the general fund.*

• *Abuse of women was forbidden, although women were taken as slaves. Those not kept for ransom were sold to the pirates as wives for the equivalent of forty dollars each.*[17]

---

14. Molly McIsaac, "Ching Shih: The Former Prostitute Turned Ruthless Pirate Who Put Blackbeard to Shame," History Daily (website), August 27, 2019, https://historydaily.org/ching-shih-the-pirate-queen.

15. Banerji, "Chinese Female Pirate."

16. "Ching Shih: Princess of the Chinese Seas," Rejected Princesses (website), https://www .rejectedprincesses.com/princesses/ching-shih.

17. "Ching Shih," Encyclopedia.com, last modified December 6, 2019, https://www.encyclopedia .com/women/encyclopedias-almanacs-transcripts-and-maps/ching-shih-fl-1807-1810.

Ching made it clear that while the pirates could take captured women as wives, they had to care for them and be faithful to them. If they raped a woman, they'd be beheaded.

It's praiseworthy that she punished rapists, but that was not an endorsement of consensual relationships between pirate and prisoner. A female prisoner who willingly had sex with a pirate to whom she was not married would be weighted down with cannonballs and thrown overboard to drown.[18] Others who didn't "listen" to the captain's orders had their ears severed, assuming that they weren't quartered or outright beheaded.[19]

Remember, these were punishments for her *followers*. When it came to her enemies, Ching was shockingly ruthless and encouraged the same tendency in her crew. When they raided cities, Ching not only tolerated killing, but rewarded crew members who returned with the severed heads of villagers.[20]

Many people decided they'd rather join Ching Shih than try to fight her. At the height of her power she commanded between twenty thousand and forty thousand people.

By 1809, her pirate raids had become so threatening that the Chinese government sent "suicide ships" to stop Ching Shih. They filled ships with explosives and launched them in the direction of her vessels. The pirates proceeded to disarm the suicide ships, repair them, and incorporate them into their own fleet.[21]

The government wasn't able to kill Ching Shih, but they were able to buy her off. When they offered payment to cease her operations, she took the money and opened a casino and brothel. She spent the rest of her life peacefully and died of natural causes at age sixty-nine.

And they say that crime doesn't pay.

---

18. Cindy Vallar, "Cheng I Sao ('wife of Cheng I')," *Pirates and Privateers* (blog), http://www
.cindyvallar.com/chengsao.html.

19. McIsaac, "Ching Shih: Ruthless Pirate."

20. Milton Meltzer, *Piracy and Plunder: A Murderous Business* (New York: Dutton Juvenile, 2001), 54.

21. "Ching Shih," Rejected Princesses.

ELEANOR DUMONT

(1834–1879)

If the saying "Lucky in cards, unlucky in love" was made to summarize anyone's life, it may well have been Eleanor Dumont.

No one knows where Eleanor Dumont, one of the more exciting figures of the Old West, was from. Her French accent may have pointed to a European birthplace or New Orleans, or just a person with a desire to stand out in rustic locations.

But everyone in San Francisco in the 1850s knew who she was.

Back then, she was known as Simone Jules. As the lone female card dealer at the Bella Union casino, she made a splash in a male-dominated world. (Fun fact: Women would not be allowed to deal at tables in Las Vegas until 1971.)[22] According to one of the gamblers, "Whatever she did, she had to be the boss."[23] By 1854 she moved to Nevada City to start her own casino, named the Vingt-et-un. She had renamed herself Eleanor Dumont, but in the years to come she would become more commonly known as Madame Moustache in reference to the sprinkling of hair on her upper lip.

The Vingt-et-un was more glamorous than anything the largely male population of miners in Nevada City had ever seen. A band played. Free champagne was passed as the men gambled. So refined was the establishment that men weren't allowed to curse inside. To people used to working in difficult, dirty, and rough conditions, it must have seemed like heaven. Whatever gold those men were able to mine, they were happy to lay down on Madame's tables.

Everything was going well. The miners were having fun, and Eleanor was making money. But if she was lucky in cards, she wasn't in love. She took a lover named David Tobin and had him assist her in the running of her operation. However, business and pleasure rarely mix, and they didn't in this case. David grew frustrated with the fact that Eleanor allowed him only 25 percent of the casino's profits.[24]

The pair split.

Eleanor decided that cards would be her true love. Well, cards and liquor. As the money dried up in Nevada City, she moved from town to town opening casinos. In the course of her travels she met some of the fabled figures of the time—it's said that in Deadwood, she taught the frontierswoman Calamity Jane how to gamble.[25]

Known for her elegant ways, Eleanor was also a formidable woman. When she saw a man cheating at one of her establishments, she beat him with a horsewhip. When a man who had lost money at her casino snapped that he suspected

---

22. Michael LaPointe, "Dice Roll: Madame Mustache," *The Daily* (blog), *Paris Review*, April 2, 2019, https://www.theparisreview.org/blog/2019/04/02/dice-roll-madame-mustache/.

23. LaPointe, "Madame Mustache."

24. Eugene Francis, "Gambling Lady," *Atlanta Constitution*, September 12, 1948.

25. Michael Rutter, *Upstairs Girls: Prostitution in the American West* (Helena, MT: Farcountry Press, 2012), 317.

she was not from a fine French family, but from Mexico, she instructed her staff to throw him through a glass door. (They were more than happy to do so.)[26] She also became known for her skills as a sharpshooter—some said that her accuracy was such that "she could plug a hole through a nickel."[27]

Strength of will and a keen eye were useful skills. Once, when Eleanor was mugged by two men she reached into her skirts, pulled out a derringer pistol, and shot them.[28]

In 1872, she sought to retire, and she bought a ranch near Carson, Nevada. There, she married a man named Jack McKnight. The marriage would prove to be her greatest error in judgment. McKnight was a con artist who quickly stole Eleanor's life savings. She proceeded to track him down and shoot him with a twelve-barrel shotgun. She was never charged with the crime, though she later admitted to it.[29] However, she was broke, with only a few jewels her husband had left behind. It wasn't enough to live on, so Eleanor sold the ranch where she'd hoped to live out her life in peace. She took to gambling once again, hoping that the tables would bring her the same luck they had in the past.

They did not.

Distraught after losing $300 one evening, she went home and drank poison. Elegant to the end, she washed it down with champagne.

Although she was gone, she was not forgotten. George A. Montrose, an editor of the *Bridgeport Chronicle-Union*, wrote at the time of her demise, "It is said that of the hundreds of funerals held in the mining camp, that of 'Madame Mustache' was the largest. The gamblers of the place buried her with all honors, and carriages were brought from Carson City, Nevada, a distance of 120 miles, especially to be used in the funeral cortege."[30]

Perhaps in the end the hand she played, if a little bloody, wasn't so bad after all.

---

26. Francis, "Gambling Lady."

27. LaPointe, "Madame Mustache."

28. Norman McLeod, "Madame Moustache," *Auburn Journal*, September 16, 1984.

29. Rutter, *Upstairs Girls*, 319.

30. Michael H. Piatt, "The Death of Madame Mustache: Bodie's Most Celebrated Inhabitant," Bodie History (website), August 2010, http://www.bodiehistory.com/madam.pdf.

GRISELDA BLANCO

(1943–2012)

JUVENILE DEATH

When people think of godfathers, they think of Marlon Brando. When they think of godmothers, they think of kindly cartoons. The latter does not describe Griselda Blanco.

The woman who would become Miami's most influential drug dealer in the 1980s was born into poverty in Colombia, where she adopted a "kill or be killed" mentality from a shockingly early age. For reference, think back to what you were doing when you were eleven years old. I'm going to say it's an age where maybe you were really into *Star Wars*, or experiencing your first crush, or from what I've seen in the movies, forming friendships that involved biking through the woods to fight killer clowns. When Griselda was age eleven, she kidnapped a wealthy ten-year-old child from an upscale neighborhood. She held him for ransom with a group of other children. When the parents did not immediately pay, the kids handed Griselda a gun and dared her to shoot the captive. She promptly put a bullet in his head.[31]

By the time she was thirteen, her kidnapping career not as profitable as she'd hoped, she began working as a prostitute. She met Carlos Trujillo around that time, a hustler with whom she had three children. They divorced by the 1970s. However, that separation wasn't sufficiently permanent for Griselda, who ordered a hit on him following a drug dispute.[32]

Then Griselda met Alberto Bravo, and her career as a drug dealer truly began. Griselda was more than willing to help Bravo. She began having special underwear made so she could smuggle cocaine when she flew to the United States.

In time, she outgrew her relationship with Alberto Bravo, as she had with Carlos Trujillo. And just as before, the two did not uncouple amicably. She felt that he had mismanaged the cocaine smuggling operation and cost her millions of dollars. One night she met him in a parking lot outside a nightclub in Bogotá. The two had words, after which Griselda pulled a gun from her boot and shot him. He returned fire with an Uzi. Griselda was shot in the stomach but recovered. Her husband, who had been shot in the face, died, as did six of his bodyguards.[33]

The incident made it very clear that Griselda was not someone to be trifled with.

In the late 1970s she moved to Miami, where she worked for Pablo Escobar's Medellín cartel. At the height of her business she was importing $80 million of product per month.

---

31. "Searching for the Godmother of Crime," *Maxim*, last modified December 14, 2015, https://www.maxim.com/maxim-man/searching-godmother-crime.

32. Leonard Greene, "Drug Thugs Kill the Queen," *New York Post*, September 5, 2012, https://nypost.com/2012/09/05/drug-thugs-kill-the-queen/.

33. "Godmother of Crime," *Maxim*.

It was a business rife with violence. That didn't seem to trouble Griselda, though. She excelled at the violent aspects of cocaine dealing that gave rise to the term "Cocaine Cowboys" around this period. Most notably she pioneered assassination by motorcycle, where hitmen would ride up alongside cars on motorcycles, shoot the target, and then speed away. It was very effective—most of the time. In 1982, one of her hits led to the accidental death of a two-year-old. Griselda was attempting to have the toddler's father killed because he'd once kicked Griselda's son.[34] The bullet meant for the father killed his child instead.

A normal person would, I suspect, be horrified by this tragedy. Not Griselda.

Jorge Ayala, the hitman who later testified against Blanco, claimed, "At first she was real mad 'cause we missed the father. But when she heard we had gotten the son by accident, she said she was glad, that they were even."[35] Again, this happened because the father had kicked Griselda's son, a relatively minor offense, so this is a grotesque idea of "even."

But Griselda's reign of terror couldn't last forever. She made too many enemies. In 1994 she was charged with three murders. She pled guilty in exchange for a reduced sentence. She left prison in 2004 and returned to her homeland, where, unsurprisingly, she was murdered. By assassins on motorcycles. Billy Corben, a director who made a documentary film about Griselda, claimed, "This is classic live-by-the-sword, die-by-the-sword. Or in this case, live-by-the-motorcycle-assassin, die-by-the-motorcycle-assassin."[36]

All things considered, her death probably deserved no more mourning than the amount she gave to her victims.

34. David Ovalle, "'Cocaine Godmother' Griselda Blanco Gunned Down in Colombia," *Miami Herald*, September 3, 2012, https://www.miamiherald.com/news/local/community/miami-dade/article1942420. html.

35. Ovalle, "Griselda Blanco Gunned Down."

36. Ovalle, "Griselda Blanco Gunned Down."

THE FEMALE PATH
TOWARD INDEPENDENCE

For most of history, cards have been stacked against women who wanted to be financially independent. Even your grandmother may remember a time when she would not have been able to have a credit card of her own.

Women who wanted to line their own coffers rather than those of their husbands faced significant obstacles.

3,100 BCE: Women in ancient Egypt have equal property rights to men. Relish this moment—it's only going to get worse.[37]

1100: Coverture, the notion that the husband and wife are one financially, is enacted in England. Married women can no longer own property or work for themselves, and their money goes to their husbands. Legally, the independence of married women ceased to exist.[38]

1753: Women in Russia gain the right to a separate economy, allowing them to work without turning all of their earnings over to their husbands.[39]

1848: The Married Women's Property Act passes in New York State. This act ensured that women had access to property they brought with them into the marriage, allowing them to rent and sell it.[40]

37. Suzanne McGee and Heidi Moore, "Women's Rights and Their Money: A Timeline from Cleopatra to Lilly Ledbetter," *The Guardian*, August 11, 2014, https://www.theguardian.com/money/us-money-blog/2014/aug/11/women-rights-money-timeline-history.

38. McGee and Moore, "Women's Rights and Their Money."

39. McGee and Moore, "Women's Rights and Their Money."

40. Jane Johnson Lewis, "1848: Married Women Win Property Rights," ThoughtCo. (website), December 1, 2017, https://www.thoughtco.com/1848-married-women-win-property-rights-3529577.

1880: On Wall Street, Mary Gage opens the first stock exchange for women.[41]

1881: Women in France are allowed to open their own bank accounts, separate from a man.[42]

1963: The Equal Pay Act passes in the United States, supposedly guaranteeing equal pay for equal work regardless of sex.[43]

1974: Until 1974, women in the United States couldn't apply for credit cards or open bank accounts without a male relative's permission, presumably because they would run up massive debt buying hundreds of hats and kittens. The Equal Credit Opportunity Act makes it illegal to refuse credit cards to women.[44, 45]

1978: The Pregnancy Discrimination Act passes in the United States, meaning companies could no longer fire women for becoming pregnant.[46]

41. McGee and Moore, "Women's Rights and Their Money."

42. McGee and Moore, "Women's Rights and Their Money."

43. "Know Your Rights: The Equal Pay Act," American Association of University Women (AAUW), https://www.aauw.org/resources/legal/laf/equal-pay-act/ November 7, 2020.

44. Natasha Turner, "10 Things That American Women Could Not Do Before the 1970s," Ms., May 28, 2013, https://msmagazine.com/2013/05/28/10-things-that-american-women-could-not-do -before-the-1970s/.

45. Brad Rosenberg, "20 Ordinary Things Women Couldn't Do in the '50s and '60s," DoYouRemember? (website), February 7, 2018, https://doyouremember.com/39730/20-ordinary-things-women-couldnt- 50s-60s.

46. Jess Catcher, "11 Ordinary Things Women Weren't Allowed to Do in the '50s and '60s," Little Things (website), https://www.littlethings.com/things-women-couldnt-do-50s/3.

KILLER
QUEENS

*"The world would be so much gentler
if it was run by women."*

—A Man Who Never Read a History Book

TOMYRIS, QUEEN OF THE MASSAGETAE
(CA. 600 BCE)

CANNIBALISM

Tomyris was not destined to be a mild and tender ruler. Her semi-nomadic tribe, the Massagetae, was known for its human sacrifice and cannibalism practices, among other things. The ancient Greek historian Herodotus wrote that "human life does not come to its natural close with this people; but when a man grows very old, all his kinsfolk collect together and offer him up in sacrifice; offering at the same time some cattle also. After the sacrifice they boil the flesh and feast on it; and those who thus end their days are reckoned the happiest."[1] A peaceful

---

1. Herodotus, "Queen Tomyris of the Massagetai and the Defeat of the Persians under Cyrus," excerpted from Herodotus, *The History*, George Rawlinson, trans. (New York: Dutton & Co., 1862), Internet Ancient History Sourcebook, Fordham University, https://sourcebooks.fordham.edu/ancient/tomyris.asp.

passing of old age was to be pitied. So Tomyris really never had any hope, as so many of us do, of dying peacefully in her own bed. Her destiny was set.

When her husband died, Tomyris was ready to show her enemies the strength and ferocity of the Massagetae. Soon after she became a widow, Cyrus the Great, the ruler of the Achaemenid (First Persian) Empire, approached her, supposedly offering marriage. Tomyris quickly and accurately assessed that Cyrus was not interested in her, but her throne.

His romantic overtures rejected, Cyrus and his army began building a bridge to cross into Tomyris's lands. When the queen saw this, she sent a message to Cyrus telling him to return to his own lands. Since that was unlikely, she also offered a battle, stating, "If you are so mightily desirous of meeting the Massagetai in arms, leave your useless toil of bridge-making; let us retire three days' march from the river bank, and do you come across with your soldiers; or, if you like better to give us battle on your side the stream, retire yourself an equal distance."[2]

Of course, Cyrus did not retreat. Instead, he devised a clever strategy. He told Tomyris he would come to her side of the riverbank. Then he sent a small number of his worst soldiers across the river. They set up a feast, "the wine cups filled full of noble liquor."[3] Tomyris's army, led by her son Spargapises, approached the feast, killed the soldiers, and delighted in the beautiful food and wine left behind.

At this point, it is important to note that, while I can think of nothing that would drive me more to alcoholic drink than ritually cannibalizing my friends and family, the Massagetae's drink of choice was goat's milk. They had no experience with liquor.[4] So, much like many inexperienced young people, the Massagetae soldiers got utterly wasted. Then Cyrus attacked with the rest of his army. He slaughtered many and took Spargapises as hostage.

Cyrus won that battle, but he would not win the war.

---

2. Herodotus, "Queen Tomyris and Defeat of Persians."

3. Herodotus, "Queen Tomyris and Defeat of Persians."

4. Princess Weekes, "Queen Tomyris of Massagetae, Slayer of Great Men & Inspiration for *Red Sonja*," The Mary Sue (website), February 21, 2019, https://www.themarysue.com/queen-tomyris-red-sonja/.

Tomyris was furious. Her message to Cyrus declared, "You bloodthirsty Cyrus, pride not yourself on this poor success: it was the grape-juice!" She told him that he could return her son and leave, and she would not kill him. However, "Refuse, and I swear by the sun, the sovereign lord of the Massagetai, blood-thirsty as you are, I will give you your fill of blood."[5]

Cyrus refused to leave. Bad decision.

Tomyris was true to her word. The two armies met in battle, and according to Herodotus, Cyrus was killed. When his body was found, Tomyris took his head and submersed it in a wine cask of blood and gore. As she did so, she said, "Thus I make good my threat, and give you your fill of blood."[6]

Cyrus the Great died at the hands of a woman more bloodthirsty than he.

How Tomyris ultimately died is unknown. I hope during the death ritual, her children washed her body down with the tiniest bit of wine. Such a woman's life surely deserved to be toasted with more than goat's milk.

5. Herodotus, "Queen Tomyris and Defeat of Persians."
6. Herodotus, "Queen Tomyris and Defeat of Persians."

BOUDICA
(30–61 CE)

RAPE + TORTURE

Everyone loves the story of a charismatic tribal leader rising up against the Roman Empire. Even the Romans loved it. Which is surprising. (Americans today definitely do not appreciate being challenged, but I suppose the confident Romans admired the moxie.)

And no woman has been more valorized for her uprising against the Romans than Queen Boudica.

Boudica became queen of the British Celtic Iceni tribe following her marriage at age eighteen to King Prasutagus. At this time, while the territories of many neighboring tribes were Roman Provinces, the Iceni's land was not, in large part because Prasutagus had established a (supposedly) firm alliance with Rome. He went so far as to "name the emperor his heir, together with his two daughters; an act of deference which he thought would place his kingdom and household beyond the risk of injury."[7]

And by all accounts that worked out just fine. Until Prasutagus died.

Then Roman centurions attacked the tribe as if they had conquered it. They drove noble members from their homes. They plundered the village. Boudica was whipped. Her two daughters were raped.

Boudica was furious.

She turned on the Roman Empire almost immediately *(as would anyone)* declaring, "Nothing is safe from Roman pride and arrogance. They will deface the sacred and will deflower our virgins. Win the battle or perish, that is what I, a woman, will do."[8]

She rode from Celtic clan to clan delivering her message of defiance. Tacitus wrote that she told each, "She was avenging, not, as a queen of glorious ancestry, her ravished realm and power, but, as a woman of the people, her liberty lost, her body tortured by the lash, the tarnished honour of her daughters."[9] Tribes were on board. Roman historian Dio estimated her forces numbered more than two hundred thousand people. Living as we do in a world where it's hard to get rapists fired from their *jobs*, let alone lead an uprising against them, that may be the most depressing part of this tale.

Gaius Suetonius Paulinus, the Roman governor of Britain, wasn't terribly worried about the revolt. He told his soldiers that "they must treat with contempt the noise and empty menaces of the barbarians: in the ranks opposite, more women than soldiers meet the eye."[10]

---

7. Tacitus, *The Annals of Tacitus*, Loeb Classical Library editions (Cambridge, MA: Harvard University Press, 1937), volume V, book XIV, http://penelope.uchicago.edu/Thayer/E/Roman/Texts/Tacitus/Annals/14B*.html.

8. Shannon Weber, *Feminism in Minutes* (London: Quercus Books, 2019), 298.

9. Tacitus, *Annals of Tacitus*, volume V, book XIV.

10. Tacitus, *Annals of Tacitus*, volume V, book XIV.

Those soldiers were about to find out women are just as capable of killing as men. Especially if those women happened to be Celtic. Boudica had grown up training with weapons, as had many other Celtic women. And in this case, they may have been especially motivated, as they were fighting to ensure that they and their daughters were not raped.

Boudica's largely female army promptly laid waste to the Roman capital of Britain, Camulodunum. They would do the same to London. And then to Verulamium. When there, they were as brutal to the Roman occupants as the Romans had been to them. Roman historian Tacitus claimed, "the British did not take or sell prisoners, or practice war-time exchanges. They could not wait to cut throats, hang, burn, and crucify—as though avenging, in advance, the retribution that was on its way."[11] It's estimated Boudica's army killed eighty thousand Romans.

Dio noted that "all this ruin was brought upon the Romans by a woman, a fact which in itself caused them the greatest shame."[12] When her gender was brought up, Boudica struck back, claiming that Rome was ruled by women, too. She said she ruled "as did Messalina once and afterwards Agrippina and now Nero (who, though in name a man, is in fact a woman, as is proved by his singing, lyre-playing and beautification of his person)."[13]

Boudica! Fun hobbies shouldn't be gendered! It's great that Nero played the lyre if that was what he enjoyed! However, everything else about Nero was *atrocious* (after murdering two of his wives, he castrated a slave who he then made pretend to be his wife), so I'm willing to let that "insult" go.

Sadly, despite her sick burns and the ferocity of her army, Boudica was not ultimately victorious. The final battle was waged in 61 CE. Although Britons outnumbered Roman troops and Boudica and her daughters drove around the

11. "Boudica (Boudicca)," Encyclopedia Romana (website), https://penelope.uchicago.edu/~grout/encyclopaedia_romana/britannia/boudica/boudicanrevolt.html.

12. Cassius Dio, *Roman History*, Loeb Classical Library edition (Cambridge, MA: Harvard University Press, 1925), volume VIII, book LXII, http://penelope.uchicago.edu/Thayer/E/Roman/Texts/Cassius_Dio/62*.html.

13. Cassius Dio, *Roman History*, volume VIII, book LXII.

battle in a chariot, shouting exhortations like "we must either conquer, or die with glory!"[14] Rome eventually triumphed.

Boudica didn't wish to live in a world ruled by Romans, stating, "Though a woman, my resolution is fixed: the men, if they please, may survive with infamy, and live in bondage."[15] She and her two daughters took poison.

Their legacy lived on. Today Boudica is remembered as an early British hero who supposedly scared Nero so much that, at least briefly, he thought of withdrawing from Britain altogether.[16] And she may have paved the way for Romans to take the women who would rise against them later (like Zenobia) a little more seriously.

14. Richard Hingley, "Big Bad Boudica United Thousands of Ancient Britons Against Rome," *National Geographic History Magazine*, October 22, 2019, https://www.nationalgeographic.com/history/magazine/2019/09-10/boudica-britain-revolt-against-rome/.

15. Hingley, "Big Bad Boudica."

16. Hingley, "Big Bad Boudica."

ZENOBIA

(240–274 CE)

Edward Gibbon claimed in *The History of the Decline and Fall of the Roman Empire* that Zenobia, the Queen of Syria, was "perhaps the only female whose superior genius broke through the servile indolence imposed on her sex."[17] This is a hilariously untrue statement, but also a stark reminder that to be considered "not servile" as a woman you have to valiantly fight basically the entire

17. Edward Gibbon, "Zenobia," from *The History of the Decline and Fall of the Roman Empire*, in *Library of World's Best Literature*, ed. Charles Dudley Warner et al. (New York: Warner Library Co., 1917), Bartleby.com, 2015, https://www.bartleby.com/library/prose/2186.html.

Roman army. A man is accorded the same amount of respect for, I'm going to say, being a manager at a local general store.

Septimia Zenobia was a remarkable person. Praise is heaped upon her by many historians. She was said not only to be very beautiful, but also to possess a brilliant intellect. She could read and write Latin, Egyptian, Syrian, and Greek. She would also prove herself to be ruthless in battle.

In 258, Zenobia married Odaenathus, the ruler of Palmyra, a province of Rome. While Odaenathus claimed to be loyal to the Roman Empire, privately he wished to become the "monarch of the East."[18] He had good reason to aspire to this position given his victory over the Persian army during this period. It is said that Zenobia's military passions were equal to her husband's and that she "appeared on horseback in a military habit, and sometimes marched several miles on foot at the head of the troops."[19] It's always nice when couples enjoy the same activities.

Zenobia might have lived out her days happily as a warlike wife. Then Odaenathus was murdered by his nephew during a coup attempt in 267.[20] Zenobia retaliated by executing his assassins. Then since their son was only one year old, she declared herself regent, claiming the title Augusta.

Then she set out to accomplish what her husband could not.

By 270 she had won a war against Egypt, beheading the Roman prefect stationed there along the way. She was not only the widow of a man who had aspired to be monarch of the East, she was also the Queen of Egypt.

Zenobia was seemingly a good ruler. One account from a contemporary says, "Her sternness when necessity demanded was that of a tyrant, her clemency when the sense of right called for it, that of a good emperor."[21]

---

18. David Hernandez de la Fuente, "Zenobia, the Rebel Queen Who Took on Rome," *National Geographic Magazine*, November 12, 2017, https://www.nationalgeographic.com/history/magazine/2017/11-12/history-queen-zenobia-defied-rome/.

19. Gibbon, "Zenobia."

20. "Zenobia," New World Encyclopedia (website), accessed January 16, 2021, https://www.newworldencyclopedia.org/entry/zenobia.

21. Linda Grant De Pauw, *Battle Cries and Lullabies: Women in War from Prehistory to Present* (Norman: University of Oklahoma Press, 1998), 75.

However, those in Rome were not fans. By taking over Egypt, Zenobia established herself as an enemy of Rome. The Roman Emperor Aurelian—himself a man so known for military prowess that his troops' battle cry was "*Mille, mille, mille occidit!*" ("A thousand, thousand, thousand he has slaughtered!")[22]—attacked Zenobia's lands.

Expecting an easy victory against a woman, Aurelian was shocked that Zenobia did not yield, even as he laid siege to Palmyra. He wrote, "There are Romans who say I am waging war against a mere woman, but there is as great an army before me as if I were fighting a man."[23]

When commanded to surrender, Zenobia contemptuously replied, "You demand my surrender as though you were not aware that Cleopatra preferred to die a queen rather than remain alive, however high her rank."[24]

This defiance would have been more impressive had Zenobia not been in the process of fleeing her capital on camelback. Aurelian captured her, and she was taken back to Rome and paraded through the streets in a celebration of Aurelian's victory.

But it was not as devastating as it sounds. She marched in the parade covered in gold and jewels. The Roman people were in awe of her. Aurelian praised her, claiming, "What manner of woman she is, how wise in counsel, how steadfast in plans, how firm towards soldiers, how generous when necessity calls, how stern when discipline demands."[25]

Rather than committing suicide and dying a queen, Zenobia married a Roman senator and lived to old age in an extravagant Roman villa. And if sometimes, from that fine house in Rome, she looked back at the days when she was Monarch of the East a little wistfully—well, who wouldn't?

---

22. de la Fuente, "Zenobia, the Rebel Queen."
23. De Pauw, *Battle Cries*, 75.
24. de la Fuente, "Zenobia, the Rebel Queen."
25. De Pauw, *Battle Cries*, 75.

CATERINA SFORZA
(1463–1509)

You have probably heard from more than one person that a woman would do anything, sacrifice *anything*, for her children.

Before you believe that, consider Caterina Sforza.

Sforza was born the illegitimate daughter to Galeazzo Maria Sforza, the future Duke of Milan, in 1463. Despite her illegitimacy, she was raised in his Milanese home, as was the custom in Italy at the time, and became one of his favorite children. Caterina grew up learning military strategy alongside her brothers. She was trained to be a warrior and intellectual, not just a wife and mother. The Sforza household contained a library of more than one thousand books. The children were raised on Cicero, Seneca, and Virgil, though Caterina's favorite was Boccaccio's *Illustrious Women*, which told stories of warrior queens like Zenobia.[26]

The inspiration gained in childhood would stay with her into adulthood.

At age fourteen, she married thirty-four-year-old Girolamo Riario, a nephew of Pope Sixtus IV. The couple made their home in a palace at Campo de' Fiori in Rome. It was described as an "earthly paradise."[27] Caterina bore six children, was beloved by the people, and rumors emerged that the Pope himself "could deny her nothing."[28]

Following Pope Sixtus's death, Caterina's situation became far less heavenly. Her husband was murdered in 1488 by the Orsi family, supporters of the new pope. His body was castrated and dragged through the streets.[29] Caterina and her children were taken prisoner. When her captors threatened to kill her, she replied, "Certainly you can hurt me, but you can't scare me, for I am the daughter of a man who knew no fear."[30] Those loyal to Caterina fled to the fortress at Ravaldino, with her instructions to hold the stronghold under all circumstances.

The Orsis were desperate to take Ravaldino. Caterina slyly offered to negotiate on their behalf, and they assented. They assumed they still had control of Caterina, for they continued to hold her children as hostages. Reportedly, as she walked into Ravaldino, Caterina flipped them the bird. They told her to surrender or they would murder her children. According to legend, Caterina stood on the ramparts, lifted her skirts to show her genitals, and screamed, "Kill them if you will, I have the means to make many more!"[31]

26. Elizabeth Lev, *The Tigress of Forlì: Renaissance Italy's Most Courageous and Notorious Countess, Caterina Riario Sforza de' Medici* (New York: Houghton Mifflin Harcourt, 2012), 3.

27. Lev, *Tigress of Forlì*, 3.

28. Lev, *Tigress of Forlì*, 79.

29. Sergio Bertelli, *The King's Body: Sacred Rituals of Power in Medieval and Early Modern Europe* (University Park: Pennsylvania State University Press, 2001), 240.

30. Lev, *Tigress of Forlì*, 129.

31. "This Renaissance Warrior Woman Defied Powerful Popes to Defend her Lands," *National Geographic History Magazine*, May 6, 2016, last modified March 15, 2019, https://www.nationalgeographic.com/history/magazine/2016/05-06/caterina-sforza/.

Considering that Caterina was thirty-six years old at the time, and women today are constantly warned that their fertility will wane after age thirty-five, I greatly admire her confidence.

Caterina won. She held off her captors long enough for her uncle Ludovico il Moro to come to her aid. Her children even survived. The Orsis didn't kill them in part because they were so bewildered by Caterina.

After recapturing her lands, Caterina declared herself regent for her eldest son Ottaviano, and she set about punishing the assassins who killed her husband. After they were hanged, their bodies were thrown to the crowd, who tore them apart. Except for the chief among them, who Caterina had bound and forced to watch the hangings. She burned his ancestral home to the ground. Then she had him tied to a horse and dragged through the town square for all to see. After the horse had made two circles, she ordered his heart to be cut out of his body.[32]

Caterina calmly walked to mass on the same street the next day.

She would marry twice more. Her lands eventually fell into the hands of the Borgias, despite Caterina commanding more than one thousand men to defend them. She was held captive by the Borgias in 1500, though they kept her in an extremely beautiful villa and endeavored to treat her more as a guest than a prisoner.

If you learn anything from these chapters, it's that men are gaga for women who successfully lead armies that kill a ton of people.

After she was released by the Borgias, Caterina lived out her days peacefully. She experimented in the field of chemistry. She eventually compiled 454 formulas into a book that was, for a long period, misattributed to Cosimo the Elder.[33] She died of pneumonia at forty-six, surrounded by her many admiring children, who remarkably did not hold that "means to make more" moment against her.

---

32. Thomas Adolphus Trollope, *St. Catharine of Siena. Caterina Sforza. Vittoria Colonna* (London: Chapman and Hall, 1859), 201.

33. Amy Lifson, "Caterina Sforza: Fearless Regent and Scientist of 15th-Century Italy," *Humanities* 38, no. 1 (Winter 2017), https://www.neh.gov/humanities/2017/winter/curio/caterina-sforza-fearless-regent-and-scientist-15th-century-italy.

MARY I OF ENGLAND

(1516–1558)

TORTURE + JUVENILE DEATH

Before "Bloody Mary" was a revolting mid-morning cocktail, the name referred to Mary Tudor.

Mary Tudor's story really begins with her father. Mary was King Henry VIII's only surviving child with his first wife, Catherine of Aragon. Catherine was a devout Catholic, which was great, as Henry was so Catholic he was called "Defender of the Faith" by the pope. But then along came Anne Boleyn. Henry wished to divorce Catherine and marry Anne, but the Catholic Church didn't allow for divorce (and, since the couple had been married for twenty-four years and had an heir, annulment wasn't an option). So, Henry broke with the Catholic Church, founded the Church of England, and made himself its head.

Henry married Anne Boleyn in 1533. In the next few years monasteries across England were disbanded, and those who remained loyal to the Catholic Church were put to death. Anne Boleyn would also be put to death for "witchcraft," but not for three years. Which, now that I type it, I realize is not a long time.

Catherine of Aragon also died in 1536. After the divorce she had been confined to a small castle. Mary had been declared illegitimate, and her birthright had passed to Elizabeth, Henry's daughter with Anne. Catherine had not been allowed to see her beloved daughter Mary, which was a cause of heartbreak for both parties.[34]

Mary responded by leaning into her Catholic faith. Doing so served both as a middle finger to the father who had disowned her and a way to maintain a connection to her mother's Spanish family. When Edward, Henry's feeble, only surviving son came to power, he publicly begged Mary to give up Catholicism. She *adamantly* refused to do so.

King Edward VI only lived to be age fifteen. That was long enough to whine about Mary still being Catholic and not much else. Through a series of extremely complicated maneuvers, Mary took command of the throne following his death.

She immediately set about attempting to undo all her father had done.

Cool! Fuck you, Dad!

In retrospect, killing three hundred Protestants might have been going a little far.

In what seems like a very pro-Mary take, History.com wonders, "But her own father, Henry VIII, executed 81 people for heresy . . . so why is Mary's name linked with religious persecution?"[35] Well, because three hundred is four times

34. Patrick Williams, *Katherine of Aragon: The Tragic Story of Henry VIII's First Unfortunate Wife* (Stroud, UK: Amberley Publishing, 2013), loc. 7197 of 9706, Kindle.

35. Una McIlvenna, "What Inspired Queen 'Bloody' Mary's Gruesome Nickname?" History.com, October 25, 2018, https://www.history.com/news/queen-mary-i-bloody-mary-reformation.

as many as eighty-one, History.com. And no one is writing books about how Henry VIII was a levelheaded man. We all agree he was very comfortable with killing people.

Soon after she took the throne, Mary married Philip, the King of Naples. She then set about rooting out those disloyal to the Catholic Church and burning them alive. Among those hundreds was Thomas Cranmer, one of the men who facilitated her father's divorce. She chose to kill him even after he recanted. Indeed, many of those "heretics" may not have been fervent Protestants at all. As Anna Whitelock wrote in *Mary Tudor: England's First Queen*, "Many of the victims were agricultural laborers and artisans denounced by their families, the victims of private grievances and local disputes."[36]

Mary's executions are memorable because so many of them were recorded in John Foxe's *Book of Martyrs*. His descriptions of "the horrible and bloudy time of Queene Mary"[37] have long lingered in the English imagination. While Foxe may have embellished some aspects, the burnings were truly gruesome. One woman, denounced by her aunt, was burned alive. No one had mentioned that the woman was pregnant. She gave birth to a baby amidst the flames. When one onlooker pulled the baby out, it was reportedly tossed back in.[38]

Mary's reign was a relatively brief five years. It was also notably without an heir. There are historians who claim if she had given birth, she might have turned England into a Catholic country once more. As she did not, the crown passed to her Protestant sister, Elizabeth.

Far from becoming a Catholic country, people in England—and indeed worldwide—began fearing that Catholic rulers might be more loyal to the pope than their own citizenry. That fear lasted for hundreds of years, far longer than burning in the streets was a possibility.

---

36. Anna Whitelock, *Mary Tudor: England's First Queen* (New York: Penguin, 2016), loc. 284 of 403, Kindle.
37. Whitelock, *Mary Tudor*, loc. xvii.
38. Whitelock, *Mary Tudor*, loc. 285.

RANAVALONA I OF MADAGASCAR

(1778–1861)

On one end of the "adopted child" continuum there is Lucy Maud Montgomery's charming fictional heroine *Anne of Green Gables*. At the other is the very real Ranavalona I of Madagascar.

Ranavalona's father was an exceedingly goodhearted minor-royal who heard of a murder plot against the king and reported it. As a reward, the king adopted Ranavalona. Years later, Ranavalona married the king's son and heir, Prince Radama. Following the king's death, she became Queen of Madagascar in 1810.[39]

---

39. Joshua, "Queen Ranavalona I: The Most Murderous Woman in History," *Historic Mysteries* (blog), June 1, 2017, https://www.historicmysteries.com/queen-ranavalona-i/.

This is already unusual because the Westermarck effect usually dictates that you do not feel sexual attraction to people you grew up with. But don't worry, the story gets weirder. Prince Radama had twelve wives. Ranavalona was not his favorite wife and she had no children with him (though it's difficult to say whether she was not his favorite because of the lack of children, or if the fact that he did not like her contributed to the lack of children). But when King Radama died at the age of thirty-six in 1828, she took the throne.

Then she killed any rivals for that throne, which meant more or less murdering her entire adopted family. Most of the male threats were speared to death. However, royal custom dictated that "royal female blood" could not be shed,[40] so Ranavalona had her female relatives starved to death. Execution of rivals was brutal, but not an uncommon occurrence. However, given that she was adopted because her father warned the king about a potential killer, there's more than a little irony to this particular turn of events.

Once she held the throne she did wonderful things—right?

Not quite.

Ranavalona was a strong and determined ruler. Upon taking the throne she declared, "Never say, 'she is only a feeble and ignorant woman, how can she rule such a vast empire?' I will rule here, to the good fortune of my people and the glory of my name! The ocean shall be the boundary of my realm, and I will not cede the thickness of one hair of my realm!"[41] To that end she took action toward insuring Madagascar's independence from imperialist rule. While her husband had been attempting to Westernize the country, Ranavalona encouraged people to celebrate their heritage and distinctive customs. Shortly after her coronation, she expelled the British representative from Madagascar. But no British occupation meant no subsidy from them, so the lost money had to be made up. So, in a terrifying decision, Ranavalona reinstituted the slave trade.

Torture during her reign was also said to be especially horrific. One of her biographers, Keith Laidler, notes that "brigands, runaway slaves or anyone suspected of traitorous leanings might be flayed alive, sawed in half, or [have]

---

40. Keith Laidler, *Female Caligula: Ranavalona, The Mad Queen of Madagascar* (Hoboken, NJ: John Wiley & Sons, 2007), loc. 444 of 2384, Kindle.
41. Laidler, *Female Caligula*, loc. 505.

their testicles crushed . . . others might be bound, then sewn into buffalo hides with only their heads protruding and hung up on poles and left to die slowly."[42] Or your lower half might be submerged in a boiling cauldron, so your genitals would be roasted while you remained alive and conscious.

It was not a great time to live in Madagascar.

Guilt was determined by a bizarre trial in which the accused was fed rice, chicken skins, and kernels of poison extracted from a tanguena bush. If the accused didn't throw up all three chicken skins, they were found guilty and executed. (Ranavalona's husband had also allowed this practice, but under his reign, dogs were permitted to stand in for their human counterparts.)

She even demanded her own lover take the test when he was said to be sleeping with another woman. He refused to submit. She proceeded to have him speared to death in his home. Supposedly, as he died, he shouted, "Glory to Ranavalona . . . live forever without misfortune!"[43] (I have said meaner things about exes who, say, failed to return some books I leant them after we broke up.)

Ranavalona did not live forever, of course, but she lived longer than her son and appointed heir might have liked. He attempted to overthrow her a few times, which only seemed to amuse her. As he plotted with Europeans, she would periodically send the military to visit him "only to have them do random, benign tasks, like picking out presents."[44]

She died peacefully in her sleep at age eighty-three. Afterward her son welcomed Europeans, abolished slavery, and instituted all manner of beneficent policies. Within a few decades Madagascar became a French colony. So, maybe she had a point about keeping Europeans out.

Her outrageous policies did not contribute "to the glory of her name," as she once hoped.

Today most people in Madagascar don't remember Ranavalona fondly. Her name is often employed as an insult.[45]

---

42. Laidler, *Female Caligula*, loc. 550.

43. Laidler, *Female Caligula*, loc. 606.

44. "Ranavalona I: The Female Caligula," Rejected Princesses (website), https://www.rejectedprincesses. com/princesses/ranavalona-i.

45. Alison Kamhi, "Perceptions of Ranavalona I: A Malagasy Historic Figure as a Thematic Symbol of Malagasy Attitudes Toward History," *Stanford Undergraduate Research Journal*, May 2002, http://web. stanford.edu/group/journal/cgi-bin/wordpress/wp-content/uploads/2012/09/Kamhi_Hum_2002.pdf.

QUOTATIONS

Have you ever noticed negative statements about female leaders in the press? It's nothing new. People have always hated it when women are in charge. To wit:

"Among the barbarians the female and the slave have the same status. This is because there are no natural rulers among them."
—Aristotle, philosopher, *Politics*, 350 BCE

"I do not permit a woman to teach or to exercise authority over a man; rather, she is to remain quiet."
—the Bible, 1 Timothy 2:12

"To promote a woman to bear rule, superiority, dominion, or empire above any realm, nation, or city, is repugnant to nature; contumely to God, a thing most contrary to his revealed will and approved ordinance; and finally, it is the subversion of good order, of all equity and justice."
—John Knox, Scottish Minister, *The First Blast of the Trumpet Against the Monstrous Regiment of Women*, 1558

"Men have broad and large chests, and small narrow hips, and more understanding than women, who have but small and narrow breasts, and broad hips, to the end they should remain at home, sit still, keep house, and bear and bring up children."
—Martin Luther, Religious reformer, *Table Talk*, 1566

"We treat women too well, and in this way have spoiled everything. We have done every wrong by raising them to our level. Truly the Oriental nations have more mind and sense than we in declaring the wife to be the actual property of the husband. In fact nature has made woman our slave."
—Napoleon Bonaparte, Emperor of France, *Memoirs*, 1831

"I'd rather travel the hardest path of matrimony than follow in your footsteps…
Get Thee Behind me, Mrs. Satan!"
—Cartoonist Thomas Nast on Victoria Woodhouse, the first female candidate
for US president, 1872

"Life's a bitch, don't vote for one."
—Anti-Hillary Clinton t-shirts popular at rallies for Donald Trump, circa 2016

"Not to be sexist, but I can't vote for the leader of the free world to be a woman."
— T.I., rapper, 2017

Section 8

BADASS WARRIORS
(NOT PRINCESSES)

*Q: "Were there female samurais?"**
A: "No. There were not. Is this a test to find out
who the insane feminists are? Aside from legend,
has any major culture had female warriors?"

—Some dude

This chapter is dedicated to the dude who posted
this. May he go unremembered by history.

---

*. Kieas, July 25, 2004, reply to Cheng, https://www.japan-guide.com/forum/quereadisplay.html?o+7443.

TOMOE GOZEN

(1157–1247)

Recent archeological digs in Japan found that approximately one-third of the bodies from a sixteenth-century samurai battleground were female. This has led historians to conclude that, "women fought in armies even though their involvement was seldom recorded."[1]

The Onna-bugeisha were formed around 200 CE, with the intention of following in the footsteps of Empress Jingū who, according to legend, led a successful invasion of Korea while pregnant. The Onna-bugeisha typically acted

---

1. Stephen Turnbull, *Samurai Women*: 1184-187 (London: Bloomsbury Publishing, 2012), 6.

as a kind of defensive squad at a time when "battles often took the form of sieges wherein the entire family would fight to defend the castle."[2] They were trained in martial arts and weaponry, especially knives and a pole arm known as the *naginata,* in the event that they had to defend their homes. Or, for that matter, their honor. It was rare for them to go on the offensive, and women who did so were known as onna-musha.

The most famous avatar for them, though there's conflict about the extent to which her story is legendary, is Tomoe Gozen (Gozen is a title which means "lady").

According to *The Tale of the Heike,* in addition to being very beautiful, Tomoe Gozen "was also a remarkably strong archer, and as a swordswoman. She was a warrior worth a thousand, ready to confront a demon or god, mounted or on foot. She handled unbroken horses with superb skill; she rode unscathed down perilous descents."[3] Little wonder, then, that her lover, Lord Kiso no Yoshinaka, made her his commander-in-chief. "Whenever battle was imminent, Yoshinaka sent her out as his first captain, equipped with strong armor, an over-sized sword, and a mighty bow; and she performed more deeds of valor than any of his other warriors."[4]

His faith was validated by her exploits. In 1181 at the Battle of Yokotagawara she beheaded seven mounted opponents. In 1183 she led one thousand warriors to victory.[5] Her tales of glory only came to an end in 1184 at the Battle of Awazu. Yoshinaka was in battle against his cousin Minamoto no Yoritomo. Outnumbered 300 to 6,000, for once Tomoe and her forces would not emerge victorious. Finally, when only five of them remained alive (of course Tomoe was one of the five), Yoshinaka told her, "You are a woman, so be off with you; go wherever you please. I intend to die in battle or to kill myself if I am wounded.

2. Rochelle Nowaki, "Women Warriors of Early Japan," *Hohonu* 13 (2015), 63, https://hilo.hawaii .edu/campuscenter/hohonu/volumes/documents/WomenWarriorsofEarlyJapanRochelleNowaki.pdf.

3. Helen Craig McCullough (trans.), *The Tale of the Heike* (Stanford, CA: Stanford University Press, 1988), 291.

4. McCullough, *Tale of the Heike,* 291.0.

5. Chelsea Bernard, "Tomoe Gozen: Badass Women in Japanese History," Tofugu (website), June 12, 2014, https://www.tofugu.com/japan/tomoe-gozen/.

It would be unseemly to let people say, 'Lord Kiso kept a woman with him during his last battle.'"[6]

Tomoe had no interest in retreating. Sighing, she declared wistfully, "Ah! If only I could find a worthy foe! I would fight a last battle for my Lordship to watch."[7] No sooner did she make that statement than thirty riders emerged, led by the fearsome Honda no Morishige of Musashi. She rode toward him, grabbed his head, and broke his neck. Then she severed it—yet another one of her many trophies. Only then did she ride off into the sunset. Or, I suppose, the sunrise, as *The Tale of the Heike* states she disappeared into "the east."

Despite her willingness to charge into death, Tomoe survived for a long time. There are legends about how she became a concubine (to produce strong sons) and other claims that she committed suicide. The least hyperbolic account claims she became a nun and lived until she was ninety years old. The memory of her has lived on far longer.

---

6. McCullough, *Tale of the Heike,* 292.0.

7. McCullough, *Tale of the Heike,* 292.

NANSICA
(DIED 1890)

ENSLAVEMENT + RAPE

Following the celebrated release of the movie *Black Panther*, the right-wing pundit Ben Shapiro angrily tweeted, "Wakanda does not exist." He was, I suppose, correct, because people with superpowers *are* imaginary. But one part of the film was strongly inspired by a largely forgotten part of history: the all-female army.

Just as portrayed in Wakanda, a military composed solely of women existed in the African Kingdom of Dahomey through the nineteenth century. During the 1840s, the female army corps numbered around six thousand.[8] It is

8. Mike Dash, "Dahomey's Women Warriors," *Smithsonian Magazine,* September 23, 2011, https://www.smithsonianmag.com/history/dahomeys-women-warriors-88286072/.

likely the women needed to serve because so many men had either died in battle or been enslaved, but women were excited to take on the position. The female warriors were known as N'Nonmiton, which meant "our mothers" in their native language.[9]

Training to become a N'Nonmiton was brutal. Candidates were expected to scale hedges of thorns. They were also left alone in the wilderness to survive for more than a week with barely any provisions. The British struggled to reconcile the fact that such a formidable army could be made up of women, with one British explorer noting in 1863, "Such was the size of the female skeleton and the muscular development of the frame, that in many cases, femininity could be detected only by the bosom."[10] Their French enemies were quick to acknowledge that the N'Nonmiton "fight with extreme valor, always ahead of the other troops. They are outstandingly brave . . . well trained for combat and very disciplined."[11]

If gaining a place in the female regiment was arduous, with it came great acclaim. The women were lodged in palatial surroundings and given plentiful food and drink. When they went out in public they were preceded by a bell ringer. When men heard the bell, they were expected to run the other way and avert their eyes. Even gazing upon the women was forbidden, and touching one of the warriors could mean punishment by execution.[12]

One way in which the women trained for combat was by executing prisoners of war. They were expected to be able to do so with one quick blow from their machete. One woman called to kill a male prisoner was Nansica. She was said to be a "ravishing girl" who had "not yet killed anyone."[13] She then "walked jauntily up to the victim, swung her sword three times with both hands, then

9. Farida Dawkins, "Dahomey Amazon Warriors in *Black Panther* to come to life again on screens," *Face2Face Africa*, March 2, 2018, https://face2faceafrica.com/article/dahomey-amazon-warriors-black-panther-come-life-screens.

10. Johanna Gohmann, "The Real-Life Women Warriors Who Inspired Black Panther's Dora Milaje," *Bust Magazine*, June/July 2017, https://bust.com/general/193143-female-warriors-of-dahomey.html.

11. Dash, "Dahomey's Women Warriors."

12. Dash, "Dahomey's Women Warriors."

13. Stanley B. Alpern, *Amazons of Black Sparta: The Women Warriors of Dahomey*, second edition (New York: New York University Press, 1998), 103.

calmly cut the last flesh that attached the head to the trunk."[14] Accounts claim that following this execution, she proceeded to wipe the blood from her weapon and drink it. Others assert that she waved her sword proudly before the crowd.

Nansica's pride was short-lived, however. She was killed three months later in battle against the French army, during the First Franco-Dahomean War of 1890. Jean Bayol, the same French chronicler who had recorded Nansica's execution of the male prisoner, came upon her in the battlefield and wrote, "She wore a white cap, scarlet pants covered by a snug pagne, a flowered vest, which, partly open, let one glimpse the nascent and pure shapes of the Dahomean vessel. The cleaver, with its curved blade, engraved with fetish symbols, was attached to her left wrist by a small cord and her right hand was clenched around the barrel of her carbine."[15] Given that men weren't even allowed to look upon the N'Nonmiton in life, I suspect Nansica wouldn't have *loved* Bayol's weird objectification of her slightly revealed body in death.

The N'Nonmiton lost that battle in large part because the French had far superior guns to the Dahomeans. When the battle against the French came to an end, the N'Nonmiton were the last to surrender. *Smithsonian Magazine* wrote that when they were finally taken by the French, "each allowed herself to be seduced by a French officer, waited for him to fall asleep, and then cut his throat with his own bayonet."[16]

The French fault was in still seeing them as women first, rather than as warriors. Very, very real warriors.

---

14. Alpern, *Amazons of Black Sparta*, 103.
15. Alpern, *Amazons of Black Sparta*, 194.
16. Dash, "Dahomey's Women Warriors."

NADEZHDA VASILYEVNA POPOVA
(1921–2013)

Not all witches fly on brooms. Some had airplanes.

Look to the Soviet squadron the Nazis called "Night Witches." This group of female aviators dropped twenty-three thousand tons of bombs on Nazi targets during World War II.[17] Indeed, they were so successful that the Nazis were convinced the Soviets had conducted experiments to somehow give the women special night vision. Any Nazi who managed to kill a Night Witch received an Iron Cross.

---

17. Brynn Holland, "Meet the Night Witches: The Daring Female Pilots Who Bombed Nazis by Night," History.com, June 7, 2019, https://www.history.com/news/meet-the-night-witches-the-daring-female-pilots-who-bombed-nazis-by-night.

And to think the Soviets had barely even given the women planes.

The 588 Night Bomber Division, comprised entirely of women (down to the mechanics), was established in 1941, at the female navigator Marina Raskova's request. Resources were scant. The women wore hand-me-down uniforms and boots from male soldiers that were much too large for them. Many of the Soviets' better planes had been lost to the war, so the women's unit was equipped only with tiny wooden biplanes from the 1920s.[18] In part to annoy the male counterparts who felt women shouldn't be engaged in battle, the women painted feminine iconography like flowers on the sides of their planes. Instead of radar, which male squadrons received, the female pilots were made to use maps and compasses.[19]

The planes' age turned out to be something of a benefit. "The planes were too small to show up on radar . . . [or] on infrared locators. . . . They never used radios, so radio locators couldn't pick them up either,"[20] noted the author and screenwriter Steve Prowse. The only indication the Nazis had that the Night Witches were coming was the sound of their planes approaching, which Nazis likened to the sweep of a broom. The Nazis agonized that the women were "precise, merciless, and came from nowhere."[21]

No one was more precise and merciless than Nadezhda Vasilyevna Popova. Born in a small town in the Ukraine, she claimed that in her youth, "I was bored. I wanted something different."[22] She found it when a plane crash landed in her town. She recalled later, "I had thought only gods could fly."[23] She enrolled in a

18. David Childs, "Nadezhda Popova: Soviet Pilot known as 'the Night Witch,'" *Independent* (London), July 16, 2013, https://www.independent.co.uk/news/obituaries/nadezhda-popova-soviet-pilot-known-as-the-night-witch-8711677.html.

19. Eric Grundhauser, "The Little-Known Story of the Night Witches, an All-Female Force in WWII," *Vanity Fair*, June 25, 2015, https://www.vanityfair.com/culture/2015/06/night-witches-wwii-female-pilots.

20. Holland, "Meet the Night Witches."

21. Childs, "Nadezhda Popova."

22. Douglas Martin, "Nadezhda Popova, WWII 'Night Witch,' Dies at 91," *New York Times*, July 14, 2013, https://www.nytimes.com/2013/07/15/world/europe/nadezhda-popova-ww-ii-night-witch-dies-at-91.html.

23. Emily Langer, "Nadezhda Popova, Celebrated Soviet 'Night Witch' Aviator of World War II, dies at 91," *Washington Post*, July 13, 2013, https://www.washingtonpost.com/world/europe/nadezhda-popova-celebrated-soviet-night-witch-aviator-of-world-war-ii-dies-at-91/2013/07/13/5561fb1a-ea3c-11e2-a301-ea5a8116d211_story.html.

flight club at age fifteen and in flight school at age eighteen, and she joined the 588th Regiment at age nineteen. She wanted to fly for the Army for very personal reasons; her brother had been killed by Nazis, and her family's home had turned into a Gestapo station.

The Nazis could hardly have found a more ruthless opponent. During her first mission, her plane was shot down and two of her fellow pilots died. She immediately flew another mission, declaring, "it was the best thing to keep me from thinking about it."[24] She would go on to fly a total of 852 missions.

She watched many friends die. She recalled later in the *Moscow Times* that "if you give up nothing is done and you are not a hero. Those who gave in were gunned down and they were burned alive in their craft as they had no parachutes."[25] The government really, really should have given them better equipment.

Nadezhda Vasilyevna Popova was awarded the title of Hero of the Soviet Union, the nation's highest honor. She also received the Gold Star, the Order of Lenin, and the Order of the Red Star. Following the war, she married another fighter pilot and settled down to a more peaceful life as a flight instructor.

It seems not only gods can fly. Women can, too.

24. Martin, "Nadezhda Popova, WWII 'Night Witch.'"
25. Langer, "Nadezhda Popova, Celebrated Soviet 'Night Witch.'"

REBELLIONS LED BY WOMEN

There is no shortage of women who thought they could change the world by straight up rebelling against authorities:

SANKT JAN SLAVE REBELLION,
1733

Slave rebellions in the Caribbean were not uncommon. Although only one in Haiti achieved freedom for enslaved people, that didn't stop many others on different islands from rising against their oppressors. The participants were often erroneously assumed to be all males, but not only did women join in these revolts, they sometimes led them. That misogynistic assumption meant that the governor of Sankt Jan in the Danish West Indies (now St. John, United States Virgin Islands) was surprised to find "one of the leaders of the rebellion, Baeffu [sic], whom none of us knew, and whom we assumed to be a man having murdered my son Pieter Krøyer and his Wife, is a woman!" In 1734, after the rebellion failed, Breffu took her own life, preferring death to enslavement.

FIGHT AGAINST BRITISH
COLONIAL POWER IN INDIA,
1780

The Indian queen Rani Velu Nachiyar watched British Imperialists kill her husband in 1772. After escaping with her daughter, she plotted revenge. In 1780 she organized a successful rebellion notable for a suicide mission in which her adopted daughter (and army commander) Kuyili covered herself in ghee, lit herself on fire, and walked into a British ammunitions storehouse.[26] Following the

---

26. "Tamil Nadu to Build Memorial for Freedom Fighter Kuyili," *Times of India*, May 16, 2013, http://timesofindia.indiatimes.com/articleshow/20075937.cms?utm_source=contentofinterest&utm_medium=text&utm_campaign=cppst.

victory, Velu Nachiyar established a woman-only army known as Udaiyaal in memory of the women who had died fighting the British.[27]

WOMEN'S MARCH ON VERSAILLES,
1789

By 1789, a single loaf of bread in France could cost as much as four-fifths of a woman's daily earnings.[28] Infuriated, and dismissing the men as cowards, women marched thirteen miles from Paris to the royal palace of Versailles wielding whatever weapons they could find. They forced King Louis XVI to return to Paris and submit to the judgment of the Revolution. This did not work out well for him! But then, the revolution did not work out especially well for women either. Within a few years, they would be dismissed by their male counterparts as hysterics who didn't embody the "masculine virtue" of the Revolution.

TIBETAN FREEDOM FIGHT,
1958

Ani Pachen, a Buddhist nun whose adopted name translated to "Nun Big Courage,"[29] led six hundred resistance fighters against the Chinese government after they began destroying Buddhist monasteries. Captured in 1960, she was imprisoned for twenty-one years, during which time she was forced to live in a pit filled with feces. She speaks of taking comfort when she was able to find a worm in the dirt. After her release she traveled the world discussing the Tibetan cause. Today, she is known as Tibet's Joan of Arc.

---

27. "Remembering Queen Velu Nachiyar of Sivagangai, the First Queen to Fight the British," TheNEWSMinute (website), January 3, 2017, https://www.thenewsminute.com/article/remembering-queen-velu-nachiyar-sivagangai-first-queen-fight-british-55163.

28. David Mountain, "The Women's March on Versailles," AreWeEurope, https://magazine.areweeurope.com/stories/silentrevolutions/david-mountain-the-women-of-the-french-revolution.

29. Douglas Martin, "Ani Pachen, Warrior Nun in Tibet Jail 21 Years, Dies," New York Times, February 18, 2002, https://www.nytimes.com/2002/02/18/world/ani-pachen-warrior-nun-in-tibet-jail-21-years-dies.html.

AVENGING
ANGELS

Look, they had a really good reason.

CHARLOTTE CORDAY

(1768–1793)

Splish, splash, Marat was taking a bath, and then Charlotte Corday stabbed him in the heart with a butcher knife. It still makes for one of history's more surprising assassinations.

Jean-Paul Marat was a journalist during the French Revolution. He ran a paper titled *L'Ami du Peuple* ("The Friend of the People"). His paper advocated Jacobin ideals. Those ideas were aligned with the laboring poor, which is all well and good, but the Jacobins also advocated radical violence against "enemies of the Revolution," which led to the Reign of Terror.

During that period, which lasted from September 1793 to July 1794, approximately seventeen thousand people met their death at the guillotine, but it's estimated that the total death toll of those killed without trial might be closer to forty thousand.[1] Those victims were not only aristocrats of the ancient regime, but also religious figures, dissident thinkers, political opponents, and honestly just about anyone who was less than enthusiastic about killing people without a proper trial.

For someone writing a book about interesting people who murder, I am surprisingly opposed to the Jacobins' approach to revolution. So was Charlotte Corday. Charlotte was the daughter of minor aristocrats. She was a member of the Girondists, a moderate faction who sympathized with the royals. She sensed that Marat and his ideas would lead to terrible bloodshed. Thus, she resolved to assassinate him.

On July 13, 1793, the day before Bastille Day, she approached Marat's house, where she was first turned away. Marat was ill and soaking in a tub to treat his degenerative skin condition. However, later in the day, she promised information that could be useful against the Girondists, and she was allowed to see Marat in his bath.

There, she plunged a six-inch knife directly into his heart. She was apprehended immediately. At her trial, Charlotte asked for no mercy, declaring, "I killed one man to save a hundred thousand." She was guillotined four days later. According to Thomas Carlyle, she went to her death "so beautiful, so serene, so full of life."[2]

That's certainly very brave. Though if anyone thinks of this as a fine example of the thought experiment of "killing Baby Hitler to prevent the Holocaust," they would do well to remember the date—right before Bastille Day—on which Charlotte killed Marat. The Terror would reach its apex in the year to come, with people's sense that Marat was a martyr as one of the

---

1. Jonah Walters, "A Guide to the French Revolution," *Jacobin*, July 14, 2015, https://www.jacobinmag.com/2015/07/french-revolution-bastille-day-guide-jacobins-terror-bonaparte/.

2. Thomas Carlyle, *The French Revolution. A History*, vol. 3 (London: Chapman and Hall, 1873), 146.

animating forces behind it. Contrary to her intent, Charlotte may not have saved one hundred thousand lives at all, instead bringing about the death of forty thousand.

CELIA, A SLAVE

(CA. 1836–1855)

Much of history is written by men. Men sitting around, asking, "Are women people? Like, in the way men are people—with all those rights?" And often they decide the answer is "No." Especially when it comes to Black women in America.

Celia was born enslaved in Audrain County, Missouri. In her early life she may have worked as a cook on a plantation. In 1850, at age fourteen, she was purchased by a sixty-year-old Missouri farmer named Robert Newsom. His wife had died the prior year, and he was eager for a sexual partner.

He raped Celia immediately after he purchased her, while on the way back to his farm. He would do so more or less continually for the next five years. Infuriatingly, this wasn't uncommon. One historian cited in Melton A. McLaurin's biography of Celia noted that "virtually every known nineteenth-century female slave narrative contains a reference to, at some juncture, the ever-present threat and reality of rape."[3]

Celia would bear Newsom two children in the years to come. By 1855 she had formed a relationship with a fellow enslaved man by the name of George, but it was short lived. Celia became pregnant once again, and George, upset that she could not tell him who had fathered the baby, asserted that he would "have nothing more to do with her if she did not quit the old man."[4]

To rebuff Newsom, Celia doubtless knew, would be nearly impossible. The attempt could result in harsh physical punishment or her being sold away from her children. Fleeing while pregnant with children in tow would be similarly difficult. However, to *not* find a way to stop Newsom's continual abuse would continue to harm her safety and sanity in addition to depriving her of a relationship with George, which was likely a rare source of happiness in her life.

Celia implored Robert's grown children by his wife to stop their father from raping her. Being financially dependent on him, or maybe just indifferent to Celia's plight, they did not take action. Finally, on June 23, 1855, she confronted Newsom directly. She told him that she would strike at him if he continued the abuse. He refused her request and announced he was "coming to her cabin that night."[5]

So Celia took a large stick to bed with her. When Newsom arrived, she beat him to death with it. For nearly an hour she watched over the body to make sure he was really dead, considering what to do. Finally, she tossed his body into her cabin's fireplace along with the stick. By morning, he had been reduced to a heap of bones, which she paid a younger slave (in walnuts) to carry out of her cabin.

Newsom's family began to search for him. It was George who pointed them toward Celia. I am not sure if George knew the extent of Celia's action,

3. Melton A. McLaurin, *Celia, A Slave* (Athens: University of Georgia Press, 2011), 24.
4. McLaurin, *Celia*, 30.
5. McLaurin, *Celia*, 32.

but I do know that George's demands were one reason she was in this situation. I'm sure George had his reasons for telling Newsom's family how to find her, but Jesus Christ, what a terrible thing to do.

While Celia initially denied any knowledge, it didn't take long for Robert's daughter to find remnants of her father's bones in Celia's fireplace, as well as buttons from his clothing.

A court trial, *State of Missouri v. Celia, a Slave*, ensued. In 1855, the law stated that it was a crime "to take any woman unlawfully against her will and by force, menace or duress, compel her to be defiled."[6] The question was whether that statute applied to enslaved women. If it did, it had the potential to topple the institutions of slavery, as it would pave the way toward granting enslaved people bodily autonomy. If it didn't, then Celia would be found guilty of murder.

Despite the attempt of Celia's counsel to use that law in her defense, the trial judge told the jury to assume the phrase "any woman" applied only to white women. The all-white, all-male jury found Celia guilty. The judge ordered that she "be hanged by her neck until dead."[7]

Only then did Celia attempt to escape. She fled the jail but was quickly captured. Despite the best efforts of abolitionists, her sentence was carried out. The night before she was hanged, she claimed, "as soon as I struck him the Devil got into me, and I struck him with a stick until he was dead."[8]

I don't think that was the devil. Celia had every right to defend herself, because despite what the judge and jury thought, she was a woman deserving of rights over her own body. Knowing that means you are human.

---

6. DeNeen L. Brown, "Missouri v. Celia, a Slave: She Killed the White Master Raping Her, Then Claimed Self Defense," *Washington Post*, October 19, 2017, https://www.washingtonpost.com/news/retropolis/wp/2017/10/19/missouri-v-celia-a-slave-she-killed-the-white-master-raping-her-then-claimed-self-defense/.

7. Brown, "Missouri v. Celia."

8. Douglas O. Linder, "The Trial of Celia: A Chronology," Famous Trials (website), https://famous-trials.com/celia/181-chronology.

MARIE SUKLOFF

(1885–?)

TORTURE

Jews have been oppressed through much of history. Like many persecuted people, occasionally they have fought back.

Marie Sukloff retaliated with a vengeance.

Marie grew up very poor on a Russian farm. She worked in a simple grocery store,[9] but she took an interest in politics. In 1898, when local men went on strike for a ten-hour workday, thirteen-year-old Marie joined them, much to the men's surprise. Afterward, a rabbi's daughter taught her how to read, as well

---

9. Marie Sukloff, *The Life-Story of a Russian Exile*, trans. Gregory Yarros (New York: The Century Co., 1915), 10, https://babel.hathitrust.org/cgi/pt?id=mdp.39015012255363&view=1up&seq=24.

as other subjects like history, geography, and the political situation in Russia at the time.

As she studied and then became a member of the Socialist Revolutionary Party, she came to know more about the ways people in power abused the Jews in Russia. Marie wrote in her autobiography of starving peasants being flogged or shot. She talks of how one wealthy townsman attempted to bury her sister alive. And of how other peasants were locked in barns and left to starve for not minding animals closely. It was a brutal time.

In her book Marie also tells of how Governor General Fyodor Dubasov had a particularly heinous reputation for carrying out pogroms. The Socialist Revolutionary Party decided to attempt to assassinate him, deeming it necessary "as a response to all the atrocities he has committed in the village. It has also become known to the committee that the governor is trying to organize a Jewish pogrom in the city of Tchernigoff."[10] Marie wanted to be involved in the attempt. She steeled herself for the act by "making a list of the Governor's victims. I read and re-read a thousand times the narratives of the peasants about his terrible crimes, and my heart bled for them."[11] She wrote that as she waited, "I sat near the window and looked at the snow-covered road. There was only one thought in my mind: he must die. All doubts had disappeared. I knew, I felt that it was going to happen."[12]

Her comrade, Nicholai, was the one who threw the bomb under the carriage. Before he did so he warned Marie to keep her distance, in case anything went wrong and she needed to continue on carrying out the murder. It was wise advice. Nicholai's bomb failed to explode, and the police riding alongside the Governor's carriage apprehended him immediately. Marie ran forward with her bomb, which she hurled directly into the carriage, knowing that doing so probably meant death for her as well as the Governor General.

---

10. Sukloff, *Life-Story of a Russian Exile*, 138.2.

11. Sukloff, *Life-Story of a Russian Exile*, 140.4.

12. Marie Sukloff, "Marie Sukloff: The Story of an Assassination (1914)," trans. Gregory Yarros (1914), website of Paul Brians, Washington State University, https://brians.wsu.edu/2016/11/07/marie-sukloff-the-story-of-an-assassination-1914/.

Later she recalled, "A terrific force instantly stunned me. I felt that I was lifted into the air."[13] Battered though she may have been, she survived. After the assassination, she wrote that "when I regained consciousness and opened my eyes there was nobody around. I lay on the road amid a heap of debris. Blood was streaming down my face and hands."[14] Governor Dubasov did not fare as well—he died as a result of injuries from the bombing.

Marie ended up, unsurprisingly, in prison and was sentenced to death. As a rule, you do not get away with suicide bombings even if you have a very good reason for carrying them out.

However, in Marie's case, that sentence was commuted to forced labor in Siberia. She would go on to escape from there and tell her story. She would be remembered not just for her own words, but those of the poet Max Eastman, who wrote "To Marie Sukloff—An Assassin," pondering, "Was it God's breath, Begetting a savior, that filled you with Death?"[15] Maybe it was God. But I'm inclined to believe that either the credit or the shame from being a murderer belonged to Marie alone.

---

13. Sukloff, "Marie Sukloff."

14. Sukloff, "Marie Sukloff."

15. Max Eastman, "To Marie Sukloff—An Assassin," *HePo*, https://hellopoetry.com/poem/73806/to-marie-sukloff-an-assassin/.

SHI JIANQIAO
(CA. 1905–1979)

TORTURE

Assassins do not typically devise a press plan to immediately and politely explain their actions to onlookers, but most are clearly not as organized as Shi Jianqiao. Though Shi likely thought of herself less as a successful assassin and more as "a good daughter."

She was born in the city of Tongcheng in China. Back then, she was known as Shi Gulan. Her father was a military officer, which was a source of great pride to their family. Shi was brought up to be a good Chinese daughter of the period, which meant her feet were bound and she received instruction from private tutors at home.[16] She was an obedient daughter in a time and a place where that was extremely important.

Shi Jianqiao could easily have grown up to be a good wife and mother and utterly unremembered by history had her father not encountered a warlord by the name of Sun Chuanfang during a battle between warlord cliques in 1925. Jérôme Bourgon, a researcher at the Institut d'Asie Orientale, notes that Sun Chuanfang "embodied the worst outrages of the warlords: fierce repression of workers' strikes in Shanghai, opium trafficking, collaboration with the Japanese."[17]

As a military officer, Shi Jianqiao's father, Shi Congbin, was decapitated by Sun Chuanfang, and his head was mounted upon a pike and displayed at a local train station. His daughter was horrified—and filled with a passionate desire for revenge. It would take her ten years to enact her plan.

Initially she was hopeful that male relatives would avenge the death.[18] She married Shi Jinggong, hoping he might exact revenge.[19] However, she ultimately found the duty fell to her. During those years she changed her name to Shi Jianqiao, the characters of which mean "raised sword."

In 1935, she enrolled her son in the same school as Sun Chuanfang's child. From there, it was easy to find out more information about his schedule, like the fact that he regularly went to a Buddhist temple. She followed him and shot him while he was praying.

16. "Sun Chuanfang, the Republic of China Female Assassin Shot Dead: Thunderbolt Means and the Heart of Buddha," BestChinaNews (website), July 26, 2016, http://www.bestchinanews.com/History/994.html.

17. Jerome Bourgon, review of *Public Passions: the Trial of Shi Jianqiao and the Rise of Popular Sympathy in Republican China*, by Eugenia Leansa, *China Perspectives*, 2008/3 (2008), https://doi.org/10.4000/chinaperspectives.4273.

18. "Sun Chuanfang," BestChinaNews.

19. Eugenia Lean, *Public Passions* (Berkeley: University of California Press, 2007), 27, https://content.ucpress.edu/pages/10541/10541.ch01.pdf.

And then she immediately distributed pamphlets which read:

Gentlemen take note:
1. Today, Shi Jianqiao (given name Shi Gulan) has killed Sun Chuanfang in order to avenge the death of her father Shi Congbin.
2. For concrete details of the situation, please refer to Gao guoren shu.
3. I have accomplished the great revenge and am immediately turning myself in to the courts.
4. As for splattering blood onto the walls of the Buddhist hall and shocking everyone, my deepest apologies.
— Female avenger, Shi Jianqiao[20]

That fourth point is as polite as the signature is badass.

In the pamphlets she also included a poem about her dedication to avenging her father, which she wrote in the classical Chinese style of seven-character, regulated verse.

I dare not forget the revenge of my father for a single moment;
It breaks my heart to watch my mother's temples turn gray.
I am loath to let her suffer any longer,
The opportunity should not be squandered.
I cannot bear to look back to ten years ago.
Things have remained the same, only the scenery has changed.
I arrive at the Society not to find the Buddha, I seek death,
not immortality.[21]

People loved the messages. Moreover, they loved her. Though a trial commenced promptly on November 21, 1935, eight days after the assassination, and there was little doubt in anyone's mind who killed Sun Chuanfang, Shi Jianqiao

---

20. Lean, *Public Passions*, 22.
21. Lean, *Public Passions*, 21.

was largely depicted positively. The professor Qiliang He wrote, "Shi Jianqiao managed to paint herself as a female knight-errant who avenged her father's death to uphold the state sponsored idea of filial piety."[22]

Shi was pardoned, and poems, stories, and novels were written in which she was depicted as the heroine. She became a widely admired symbol of honor and was elected as vice-chair of the Women's Federation of Suzhou in 1949, fifteen years after the killing. She lived quite peacefully until her death from natural causes in 1979.

If you're going to kill anyone, remember to write a nice poem first.

---

22. Qiliang He, "Scandal and the New Woman: Identities and Media Culture in 1920s China," *Studies on Asia*, series IV, vol. I (Fall 2010), https://web.archive.org/web/20120912133650/http://studiesonasia.illinoisstate.edu/seriesIV/documents/Qiliang_HE.pdf.

VIRGINIA HALL
(1906–1982)

Virginia Hall was not who you would expect to be Britain's "most dangerous spy." She was an American. She was a woman. And she was an amputee. None of those features prevented her from killing one hundred fifty Nazis and capturing five hundred more.

Virginia was born in Maryland to a wealthy family. Her father was a banker who also owned cinema houses. Her mother was described as "snooty."[23] That characteristic did not define Virginia. From early in her life she was *awesome*.

---

23. Sonia Purnell, *A Woman of No Importance: The Untold Story of the American Spy Who Helped Win World War II* (NewYork: Viking, 2019), 12.

She once wore a bracelet made of live snakes to school.[24] She loved hunting, and her father bought her a gun at a young age. She studied French at George Washington University and hoped to become a diplomat. This was a daunting goal, for after applying to work in the Foreign Service, she found out that only six of fifteen thousand Foreign Service officers were women.[25] Sadly, Virginia would not be among them, but she did secure a job as a clerk at the American embassy in Warsaw.

From Warsaw she shifted to the embassy in Turkey. It was there, at age twenty-seven, that her leg was amputated after she developed gangrene following a hunting accident. Though this was a truly terrifying experience, Virginia handled the incident with aplomb, naming her prosthesis "Cuthbert."[26]

When the Nazis rose to power in 1939, Virginia tried to volunteer for the women's branch of the British army, but she was told she wasn't a good candidate, perhaps due in part to the absence of her leg. But Cuthbert didn't stop her from going to France and driving ambulances for the French during the Nazi invasion. Once France fell, she connected with the British Secret Service section known as the Special Operations Executive (SOE). Its purpose was, according to Winston Churchill, to "set Europe ablaze"[27] through spying and subversion of native people. Virginia begged to join. Women weren't supposed to be allowed in the agency, but after six months, there were still no agents in France. Virginia promised to be, at least, not very suspicious. So, with a cover story that she was a reporter from the *New York Post* newspaper, through which she could file encoded messages in her stories, she became a rare female agent for the SOE.

Virginia was paired with a male operative, but she ditched him so she could focus on aiding members of the French Resistance. Operating under the field name Germaine Lecontre, she was trained to kill. She preferred to use what she

---

24. Greg Myre, "'A Woman of No Importance' Finally Gets Her Due," NPR, April 18, 2019, https://www.npr.org/2019/04/18/711356336/a-woman-of-no-importance-finally-gets-her-due.

25. Purnell, *Woman of No Importance*, 18.

26. "1945: Virginia Hall," Intel.gov, website of the Office of the Director of National Intelligence, November 5, 2020, https://www.intelligence.gov/index.php/people/barrier-breakers-in-history/662-1945-virginia-hall.

27. Purnell, *Woman of No Importance*, 37.

referred to as "the pills,"[28] cyanide capsules that, if broken and ingested, would bring about death in forty-five seconds. She was also prepared to take them herself if she was captured by the Nazis. Her chances of survival were estimated to be 50 percent.

She survived. During her time in France, she worked with local prostitutes who rifled through their German clients' pockets for papers and information Virginia could photograph. Her "tart friends"[29] also proved useful by taking in British airmen who had been shot down; Virginia would then help transport them out of Nazi-occupied France.

New arrivals from the SOE flocked to Virginia to "get a lay of the land." She was happy to oblige. She even went so far as to help several of her fellow agents escape from jail in 1942. After fourteen months of operation, Nazi leaders declared her "the most dangerous of all allied spies"[30] and offered rewards for her capture. Gestapo leader Klaus Barbie declared, "I would give anything to get my hands on that limping Canadian bitch!"[31] Was it a testament to Virginia's skill that he didn't even know her nationality?

Her notoriety meant she was forced to flee France, making an arduous fifty-mile trek into Spain across the mountains on foot. She wrote to her superiors that Cuthbert might be tiresome, and unfamiliar with Virginia's pet name for her artificial leg, they cabled back, "If Cuthbert is tiresome, have him eliminated."[32]

Virginia was unsatisfied in Spain, claiming, "I am living pleasantly and wasting time. It isn't worthwhile and after all, my neck is my own."[33] So she returned to France, shortly before D-Day, this time working for the American Office of Strategic Services (OSS). She disguised herself as an old milkmaid so her limp might be mistaken for an elderly woman's gait. *Smithsonian Magazine*

28. Purnell, *Woman of No Importance*, 47.

29. Purnell, *Woman of No Importance*, 75.

30. Dave Roos, "World War II's 'Most Dangerous' Allied Spy Was a Woman with a Wooden Leg," History.com, February 27, 2019, https://www.history.com/news/female-allied-spy-world-war-2-wooden-leg.

31. Roos, "'Most Dangerous' Allied Spy."

32. Purnell, *Woman of No Importance*, 98.

33. Cate Lineberry, "WANTED: The Limping Lady," *Smithsonian Magazine*, February 1, 2007, https://www.smithsonianmag.com/history/wanted-the-limping-lady-146541513/.

notes that during that period "Hall stated that her team had destroyed four bridges, derailed freight trains, severed a key rail line in multiple places and downed telephone lines. They were also credited with killing some 150 Germans and capturing 500 more."[34]

After the war, Virginia continued to be a somewhat elusive presence. She declined most interviews and didn't like to talk about her time as a spy. Nonetheless, she received some of the highest possible wartime honors from three separate countries—the Distinguished Service Cross from the United States, the Croix de Guerre from France, *and* an MBE (Member of the Order of the British Empire) in the United Kingdom. Afterward she joined the CIA, but this time she worked at a desk, putting less strain on Cuthbert. She retired in 1966.

Her memory lives on in particular with the French and British people, whose ambassadors in Washington held a ceremony in 2006 on the hundredth anniversary of her birth to honor her as "a true hero of the French resistance."[35] The CIA also named a training facility for field agents after her.

After retiring she lived on a farm with her husband, who had also been an OSS operative, until her death in 1982. I hope in those final years she found she was able to "live pleasantly" without feeling too bored, taking comfort in the great number of people her actions inspired and aided.

---

34. Lineberry, "WANTED: The Limping Lady."
35. Purnell, *Woman of No Importance*, 309.

FREDDIE OVERSTEEGEN

(1925–2018)

If when you think of "people who killed Nazis" you envision tough guys like Indiana Jones, you are missing out. Look instead to Freddie Oversteegen. This Dutch woman was only fourteen years old when she and her sixteen-year-old sister Truus joined the resistance movement in World War II. Freddie's youthful demeanor—she sported beautiful braids and rode a bicycle through town—made her inconspicuous.[36] Certainly, the Nazis occupying her hometown of Schoten

---

36. Harrison Smith, "Freddie Oversteegen, Dutch Resistance Fighter Who Killed Nazis Through Seduction, Dies at 92," *Washington Post*, September 16, 2018, https://www.washingtonpost.com/local /obituaries/freddie-oversteegen-dutch-resistance-fighter-who-killed-nazis-through-seduction -dies-at-92/2018/09/16/7876eade-b9b7-11e8-a8aa-860695e7f3fc_story.html.

didn't realize that she kept a gun in her bike basket and that she was fully prepared to kill.

Even before she joined the resistance, Oversteegen's family had sheltered Jews from the Nazis. Following the Nazi invasion of Holland in 1940, her mother made sure her girls "learned that if you have to help somebody, like refugees, you have to make sacrifices for yourself."[37] She told *Vice Netherlands* that even at her young age, she "knew a lot about what was going on." She helped her mother and sister by distributing resistance pamphlets on her bicycle. And when she found posters encouraging men to join the German army, she posted warnings over them (basically saying, "this is not a good idea").

It wasn't a surprise, then, when a commander with the Haarlem Resistance Group asked Mrs. Oversteegen for her permission to let her daughters join their group. She granted it. At that time, Freddie was only sixteen years old. In that underground movement, there were only three young women—Freddie, Truus, and Hannie Schaft, who was killed before the end of the war. Together, they would help rescue Jewish children, blow up train tracks, and of course, kill Nazis. When the resistance leader told the sisters that they would "learn to shoot, to shoot Nazis," Freddie, at least initially, responded with enthusiasm, remarking, "Well, that's something I've never done before!"[38]

The bicycles the sisters had used to distribute pamphlets would prove immensely useful. They could allow the girls to shoot Nazis and then ride away in haste. In some cases, they would meet Nazis in bars and suggest that they take a romantic walk in the woods. Once they were in a sufficiently secluded location, they'd shoot the men. Freddie was the first of the sisters to kill. As for how many times she did so, she only said, "One should not ask a soldier that."[39]

The Oversteegens were saddened and upset by their actions, but they never regretted them. Freddie claimed, "We had to do it. It was a necessary evil,

---

37. Becky Little, "This Teenager Killed Nazis with Her Sister During WWII," History.com, September 19, 2018, updated March 1, 2019, https://www.history.com/news/dutch-resistance-teenager-killed-nazis-freddie-oversteegen.

38. Ellis Jonker, "Freddie and Truus, Sisters in Arms," *Under Fire: Women and World War II*, ed. Eveline Buchheim and Ralf Futselaar (Amsterdam: Hilversum, 2014), 144, https://books.google.ca/.

39. Smith, "Freddie Oversteegen, Dutch Resistance Fighter."

killing those that betrayed good people." Truus claimed that she thought of killing Nazis as "remov[ing] tumors from society."[40] Some said that killing was wrong under any circumstances, to which Freddie replied (and I like to imagine she said this with an eye roll), "What about the six million Jews? . . . Weren't they innocent people? Killing them was no act of reprisal. We were no terrorists. The real act of terror was the kidnapping and execution of innocent people."[41] When asked how she moved on from her actions and overcame her trauma, she replied, "By getting married and having babies."[42]

If there's a difference between the Oversteegen sisters and the men of the *Inglourious Basterds* movie, it's not that they were women. It's that they existed.

40. Jonker, "Freddie and Truus," 146.

41. Sam Roberts, "Freddie Oversteegen, Gritty Dutch Resistance Fighter, Dies at 92," *New York Times*, September 25, 2018, https://www.nytimes.com/2018/09/25/obituaries/freddie-oversteegen-dutch-resistance-fighter-dies-at-92.html

42. Noor Spanjer, "This 90-Year-Old Lady Seduced and Killed Nazis as a Teenager," VICE, May 11, 2016, https://www.vice.com/en_us/article/dp5a8y/teenager-nazi-armed-resistance-netherlands-876.

ACKNOWLEDGMENTS

Unlike many of the women in this book, I did not work alone. I'm so grateful for the efforts of so many people to bring this murderous tome into the world.

I owe a huge debt of gratitude my editor, Samantha Weiner, whose excellent feedback helped refine this manuscript.

My agent, Anna Sproul-Latimer, who was enthusiastic about this project from the beginning.

My mom, who offered impressively calm suggestions while reading about women who ate people.

The illustrator, Eva Bee, whose drawings truly brought this to life.

The entire team at Abrams, who deserves credit for turning this from "me shouting about a bunch of weird murderesses I was interested in" into an actual book.

For all the weird dudes online, who believed women could not pick up a sword, you inspired this. And for all the women who wanted to make sure I was including their favorite grisly female killer, you also inspired this.

And of course, my husband, Daniel Kibblesmith. If you are ever murdered, I will avenge you, just like my hero, The Punisher.